# LALITAMBA

2015

*Lalitamba 2015*

P.O. Box 131, Planetarium Station
New York, NY 10024

ISBN 978-0-9960236-2-7

*Lalitamba* ISSN 1930-0662 is published annually in the United States by Chintamani Books. The journal is printed in accordance with the Sustainable Forestry Initiative.

Submission Guidelines: Please submit up to five poems or one work of prose per envelope. Include SASE and contact information (name, address, phone, email). Work should be previously unpublished. Address all correspondence to:

*Lalitamba*
P.O. Box 131
Planetarium Station
New York, NY 10024

Subscriptions are $12 for one year, plus $4.50 postage and handling.

Where's the masthead? In the Indian tradition, a devotee doesn't take personal credit for what is done. The devotee recognizes that all is possible through divine grace and acts as an instrument for that grace. This is why we don't list a masthead. The journal is an offering.

Lalitamba, Inc. is a 501(c)3 nonprofit organization. The journal is donated to shelters, hospitals, and prisons throughout the United States. *Lalitamba* also partners with Lalitamba Saranam, a holistic shelter serving the homeless in New York City. Proceeds from magazine sales are used for these charitable purposes. Further charitable contributions are tax-deductible. Thank you!

The name for the journal was inspired by a *bhajan* sung on a pilgrimage through India.

In early 2004, we traveled through the country with the "hugging saint" to alleviate the suffering that comes with poverty, illness, and plain loss of hope. The journal was founded upon our return to New York City, in November of that year.

The name "Lalitamba" means Divine Mother. In India, the Divine Mother is also praised as *jagado dharini,* or "She Who Sustains the Universe."

# TABLE OF CONTENTS

*Essays*



*Art*

## LETTERS AND PRAYERS. . .

Some days life is like this. Spread open, like
a blanket, like a winding sheet. Nothing's neat, the sky
an unrelenting blue. You, gone. The link to what I know

lost, fumbled, missing, strewn. Where does it go
when it's gone? What do we know about ourselves
when it disappears

like the air itself? Tracking what's there is all that's left.

Even so, in the middle of it, the sky is still precious,
inviting, a church of earth, land under me, green, brown,
black, auspicious, the smell of it is, the dirt is.

Native Americans ate dirt in order to remember their
connection to the earth.

Alleluia, I say as I walk on and on. Thank you. Tell me how
to do better. Alleluia. How to find a way back. For the old

and alone, with a single heart, let me sing in the night.
That's right.

Like a child is its mother. Thanks for the day, they say. I say.
The way out seems endless. Morning light. The aspen leaves
hanging over the window. Leaves like hearts. Alleluia.

Today I am grieved. I am thankful. I say, "May all beings
be safe and happy." Thanks for another one. The moment
right now,

alone as I might be. How far away you are. Farther
than the stars. Light years. More. More than I can calculate.
Imagine.

Thanks for the day. Alleluia. I know this is right. Singing
without reason. Tacking ground. Telling what is.
Thank you.

Charlene Langfur
Palm Springs, CA

I meditate upon you
for the removal of obstacles.
I feel the child awaken within.
Feet, eyes, trunk grow,
and I pray humbly to you
Sri Ganesh, god of humans,
reflection of my face.
As my child develops, I pray
I won't see those nodules,
though they would have made me proud, once.
Prohibit the potent accoutrement
now the surest death sentence.
Prevent the ivory weapon
certain to turn on its host.
Sri Ganesh, great god of this land,
I pray so my child may live,
a fallacy of what we once were,
representative of what we will be.
I meditate upon you
for removal of this obstacle.

*Note: A few scientists have recently claimed that elephants know they are being hunted for their tusks. They are intentionally breeding with other elephants who don't have tusks. Statistics show that fewer and fewer elephants are growing tusks.*

*With the knowledge we have of elephants, I see little evidence to deny that they are, in one manner or another, spiritual beings. There are many spiritual lessons we can learn from elephants, particularly in studying their familial bonds and the ways they grieve, which in so many ways mirror our own.*

*As elephants continue to be hunted for their tusks, I imagine that their spiritual wishes are changing as well. I worked to depict that within this prayer-poem.*

Katrina Kent
Old Orchard Beach, ME

Before the likeness of Mary,
while kneeling in this lucent candle-glow,
I pray I may perceive our God as clearly
as you, whose face shimmers in golden shadow.

This silent church, empty of those I know,
stirs me to ponder burdens that are heavy,
while kneeling in this lucent candle-glow.

Married, like you, I plead that I may grow
to honor love with the same dignity
as you, whose face shimmers in golden shadow.

As "Mom" to children, I implore you to show
me how to stand firmly, but also kindly,
while kneeling in this lucent candle-glow.

I seek strength, too, to walk the vales of sorrow
with the same patience and humility
as you, whose face shimmers in golden shadow.

The time is short. Soon I'll need to go
back to my life, which I see differently
now, praying in this lucent candle-glow
to you, whose face shines gold into every shadow.

Kenneth O'Keefe
Pittsburgh, PA

*This journal is an offering.*
*May all beings be joyful and free.*

*John Grey*

## DREAM WOMAN PLUS DOVES

A woman of plenty,
and brilliant white doves—
did I dream them, too?
It's morning.
I've graduated from sleep
with a doctorate in fantasizing.
I flex my knees, stretch my arms,
tell the mirror, "I don't want to die."
What if a dream comes true
and I'm not here to hug it to me,
look up and watch
its dazzling, soaring accoutrements.

I dreamed a face out of my shadow,
added birds like snow.
My mind's an old mansion gathering dust.
Who cleaned the windows there?
I went to bed, so I could wake up.

I was born in the busy city
but raised on solitude.
I have a human thirst
in a variety of languages.

I'm an ill-kept field.
I'm great trembling waters.
I listen to immortal asides,
a white whisper in variegated light.

Ah, my woman with your perfect shape:
not skin but subconscious,
not alive but a servant of yearning,
a heart carved from mine
alongside wings in their blue refuge—
Prayer still burns in my palms,
and hands ripple my untidy flesh.
The bed is my comfort.
I'm a child of the night long,
an image still clinging to my head,
the places where I anchor,
ephemeral and free.

*Christopher Presfield*

# PRISON CONCRETE WITH MENTORS/ SINGING

The empty page, watched
clock; how it bleeds
bad luck. Body's gray
inspiration's wasteland;
and now, sky's blue
as we imagined it—
beyond remorse, pain
of voice, as with
the sentience of time.

Faded images or tunes
dissuade the muse, kidnap
songs. While mentors die
north of hell, Lethe
churns in protest, plummets
corridors of salmon, slash,
as storms rage through all,
as skeletons react in Fukushima
and drug lords collect bones.
No purpose compels such madness.
Only art on a blue day.

The sky's lower now
than I've ever seen it,
as with ceilings
of cells. Weeks
they said; perhaps
they're gone. You go on
amidst gray, unexpected endings;
mindful of birds that sing
lost upon a thorn,
but sing still.

**Parked Truck**

David L. Gourdine

*Benjamin Nash*

# THE STATE HOSPITAL

In 1955 the Texas Ranger
walked in,
then
talked
to the men,
talked to them about the riot,
about the attempt to give the superintendent
electroshock treatment,
the abuse,

but said nothing about an all
black hospital.

In 2002 the psychiatrist on the ward
walked in,
then
talked
to the men,
talked to them about the videos
that he was going to ban, those with rap,
all the gangster elements,
the abuse,

but said nothing about my
cowboy movies.

*Benjamin Nash*

# THE MILITARY CHAPLAIN

It might be

deterrence,
integration,
interdependence,
the convergence of interests,
the accommodation of interests,
less ideological, ethnic, or religious conflict,
fear of the use of nuclear weapons,
lessons learned,
solutions,

or even

balance of power,
collective security,
international law,
respect for sovereignty,
reconciliation of differences,
institutional spaces for diplomacy,
economic development,
international consensus,
democratization,
shared norms,
statecraft,

but it is also

love,
love as the important value
that Pastor Boehlke talked about in confirmation class
in the little Lutheran school

in the city.
It is love that makes the difference.

*Kenneth O'Keefe*

# THE EFFECT OF FINDING FRAGILIITY

In time, he's gained a more awakened stage,
aware of how destructible the air
around his planet is, and how a page
if torn may not again have words to share.

In youth, he threw his weight around to get
his way. A brow-lambasting style became
his strategy. How often he was met
with fear until, at last, he shrank, ashamed.

In seeing how his brazen bulk gave pain,
he lost a lot of pounds through diets of
remorse. But while his frame has thinned, it's plain
the likeness of the lightness of God's love
won't wholly radiate through him 'til he's
made sheer as air that feeds the sun to trees.

*Vanessa Raney*

# I SAW HIM IN MY CELLMATE

i.
I was jailed once, for contempt. That cost me seven days.
I spent one day in a room with other women and a guest
speaker. We sat in chairs with hands on tables. She stood
in the front, next to a big speaker

ii.
She never let go of the microphone, told us she learned
to sing while listening to the radio, that this was God's plan
for her to come and talk to us, to let us know He still cared
for us. She singled another woman out for prayer
while I almost cried.

iii.
Yet I know God was there, because I saw Him
in my cellmate, a prostitute who gave me her chocolate
snacks when I refused to eat after I got sick from other
foods. How she kept silent until the guards came
and threatened to send me for clinical evaluation if I didn't

iv.
shower. I refused to, because I didn't want to be naked
in public again. She also chose to share her cell,
worried for my safety. Thus, for me, God is always
in the actions of other people, not words.

*Keir Weimer*

# JUST ANOTHER DAY

The wind beat rhythmically, as if the sails were hand drums. They began to luff with a rhythmic cadence.

The wind was changing direction.

At first the shift was gradual, then sudden. We needed to commence a port tack to remain on course. We were headed toward Luanda, the capital of Angola, on the southwestern coast of Africa.

We had been following the Skeleton Coast off Namibia for some time, keeping within a mile of the shore; we could inhale the exotic flora and fauna. This shift in the wind—now a steady northerly gale—would make the next leg of the voyage difficult.

As we turned toward starboard, the boom of the mono-hulled sloop flew across the deck, nearly taking me with it. We were on a close-hauled tack toward the coast, traveling at a healthy speed. The water sprayed over the bow as we cut through the swells, sending a brackish mist into my face.

The day was clear. You could feel the power of nature at work. Large birds I could not identify flew overhead. They cut back and forth over the mainsail, uninhibited. We drew closer and closer to the shore, zig-zagging deliberately before we tacked back out to sea.

I saw several animals in the distance as we approached, a flurry of activity on the cliff that abutted the sea surge. When we drew close enough, I saw the pride of lions tearing apart the carcass of some unlucky prey. There had to be at least eight of them, maybe ten. They moved quickly and were hard to count. Their frenzy was ravenous. They clawed and jabbed, moved in and out. They were beautiful, strong, and stoic creatures. They moved with confidence, with deliberation.

Captivating—these beautiful specimens of God's grandeur. At the top of the food chain, they were the rulers of their kingdom, free to roam, pursue, and indulge at will.

I was fascinated.

When I awoke from this fixation, we were close to shore. Emerging rocks in the shallow water threatened the boat. We needed to come about to a starboard tack and head back out to sea, immediately.

We prepared to come about. I threw the rudder to my right. This brought the boat turning furiously into the strong wind ahead. The boat came about, and the boom flew across the deck.

I ducked well in advance this time. The sails followed and captured the wind on the leeward side. We were headed back out to sea, away from the lions. We were vulnerable again, as we sailed into the hands of providence.

⌘

"Count time, on the count, sitting or standing," came blaring over the loudspeaker. I was wrenched from sleep, dragged down from the dream. I rose from my rack reluctantly, to meet the morose stares of sixty other men. They too had been yanked from their dreams, brought back to reality with jarring haste.

The razor wire outside the window shone with authority in the rising sun.

*I am still here. This is my life. This is the beginning of another day.*

Constriction and humility set in, the way they did every day. With the sun comes the count, the first of six daily counts taken, as if someone might manage to overcome three fences, each topped with razor-wire, motion sensors, cameras; each manned by guards in towers with scoped rifles, their rules of engagement, liberal. The count clears quickly. Another ordinary day in the prison institution has begun.

Yes, it is difficult without question to awaken to this day in and day out, but you get used to it. You get used to anything if given enough time. That's all I've got.

I got used to it, because I had no choice. Either adjust or self-destruct. Not a difficult choice. This particular day is going to be no different from any other day. As you might imagine, life in prison is quite different from life on the outside, known colloquially as life on the "streets" or in the "town."

The days are strictly regimented, without tolerance for deviation. The institution is truly a total institution. The administration is akin to one of a totalitarian regime. The individual here is subordinate to the proper functioning of the whole, that whole being the correctional organism that exists in seeming perpetuity.

The unit is alive—not flourishing, but alive. Teeth are brushed, hair is combed, and faces are shaven. The smell of cheap drip coffee brewing in the hand filter fills the air.

CNN's Headline News is covering Paris Hilton's recent run-in with the law. This time, it happened in Las Vegas. Possession of cocaine. Hardly surprising, yet thirty men stand stuck. Is this worth five minutes of above-the-fold coverage? Must be a slow news day.

Ms. T walks through the door with her usual stride, her frown on display. The dormitory porters scurry from the woodwork. They clamor for brooms, dustpans, and mops. Mr. Rogers is already buffing the recreation room. He's been buffing since six in the morning. (He's been here for years.) Beds are being made, cubes are being cleaned, and people are pulling themselves together for another day.

I find myself taking part in the same early-morning routines. When did routines become a bad thing? Oh, yeah, when I came to prison.

I take that back. There is no routine coordination and selfless camaraderie. Are we a colony of robots? Maybe.

I watch the mindless execution of an ant farm in the dormitory.

Everyone is concerned with only himself and his immediate survival needs. The next man means nothing and is of no importance.

You might wonder why this is. I still do at times. I don't think prison was always like this. In fact, I remember a few old timers at my last spot telling me that prison never was like it is today. The penitentiary has changed. There's no longer unity or solidarity.

"Get your cubes straight inside-out," broadcasts across the PA system. Ms. T gives this signature first command every morning around seven-thirty.

By this time, most cubes are pretty straight. She conducts her first patrol shortly thereafter, cube-standard tickets in hand. She writes five to ten violations on that first walk through, more if she's having a good day. The inevitable moaning follows, as if the accused didn't know what was expected of them from her posted standards or countless reminders.

The commotion and noise of the morning rush retreats, only to return. Unprogrammed inmates remain on the dormitory unit, going about their individual agendas, rather than those of the State. Chess, dominoes, and scrabble are broken out. The tables are arranged close to the TV. The trash talk begins.

"You're garbage...I'm gonna wash you up...My niece has more game than you...You clown."

The TV channel changes from news to music video reruns on MTV. The outcome of the best of twenty-one games in chess will be the highlight of the day for many.

This treading of water is unsettling, this "killing time" mentality, disturbing.

I made a commitment to myself and to others: I would make the best of this time, this time away from society, family and friends, this time away from my life. I would take the steps I needed to become a better person, to live a better life as a result of this experience.

Every morning when I wake up here, I remember that commitment, that vow I gave at my sentencing hearing before I was ushered off to prison. I have a duty, an obligation. This is not simply doing time. I must use every passing second to recover, to reach a place where I'm healthy enough to help others achieve whatever I find.

I find my way to the corner of the recreation room, right after morning chow. I've jerry-rigged a little office in this corner. I pull two tables into an "L" set-up. I sit sequestered in the corner beside one of the pay phones. I set my typewriter on one table and lay out whatever I'm working on atop the other. I have my steaming cup of Folgers instant coffee in hand. I sit down and get to work.

Reverse. I read the paper for an hour or two, then get to work. Here I sit from around seven-thirty in the morning until two in the afternoon, with a break for lunch at eleven-thirty. I get work done in this little nook, despite the surrounding confusion.

The recreation room is roughly 800 square feet. The TV is constantly on, and not simply on; the volume is turned up to the loudest it will go. This, I still don't understand. The people watching sit within ten feet of the TV.

I've gotten fairly good at tuning-out the cacophony. Again, you get used to anything. I don't have a choice, if I want to get anything done in here.

When people think of doing time in prison, they imagine downtrodden inmates sitting in cells and doing nothing. Sure, that happens. Moreso in the maximum security prisons, where the sentences are longer.

In contemporary prison, inmates are required to participate in programs, depending on the assessed need for academic, vocational, or substance abuse therapy. Often, all three are required. The day is strictly apportioned around these programs, recreation, meals, and extracurricular activities.

It's very easy for the inmates to "fake it to make it," to do the bare minimum to satisfy the "assessed need" imposed by the State's agenda. This is the *modus operandi* of the majority. Tragic.

Mid-morning, I head back to my cube for a five-minute rest. Maybe, I get another cup of mud. Maybe, I just take a cursory glance around my area—making sure things are in order.

Today, I find a yellow carbon copy of a cube standard violation on the top of my big locker.

*You gotta be kidding me. The care and attention I take to avoid this very thing. Come on.*

"Locker needs to be centered in cube between bed and partition," it reads in barely legible scratch.

My small locker had been ever so slightly askew. I'd been rummaging earlier and must have moved it.

Annoyed, I crumple up the violation—making sure Ms. T doesn't witness my disdain—and walk back out to my office. Here, I might spend the remainder of the morning doing whatever I might be doing that particular day. If I've captured the elusive muse and feel particularly creative, I'll write a short story. If I need to write an essay or response for a course, I'll open the syllabus. I may just read whichever book I am currently reading. I might catch-up on correspondence with family and friends. Maybe, it's crossword time. Maybe, I just sit and think, staring at the institutional cinder. Whatever I do, I feel most comfortable in the "office."

I cannot even call it my "office." These tables are not mine. Nothing is mine in here, really. This place is not home. This is merely where I live, for now. This is where I've been placed for what I have done.

I accept the things I cannot change. I must also find the courage and resolve to change the things I can. This is why I spend my time the way I do: I remember to live fully, each day. I awaken to the glare of razor wire lacing the landscape just outside my window, and sixty groggy faces. Awakening is one of the few choices I can make, without the State offering "guidance."

Two o'clock rolls around faster than I realize. It's ten of, and I have to get ready to go workout. I tidy-up the "office" and hurry to my cube to change.

Some of my neighbors are doing the same thing. Afternoon program run has just gone out. The dorm is relatively quiet, though it is never quiet here. Ever.

Even in the middle of the night, four or five Bunyans are chopping down sequoias. That's literally what the noise sounds like.

Had I not procured a set of earplugs on the black market, from a guy I know on the lawns and grounds gang, I'd be denied the only real peace in here—a dream state, a place where you're undisturbed for six short hours, from the last count of one day, until the first count of the next day. Sleep is the only true egress from this prison, as temporary and artificial as such an escape is.

Today, I may get pulled over *en route* to the yard for my workout, or I may not. A random search takes place. They say the search is random, but if it's so random, why do the same people get pulled over and frisked? Young, muscular black men stand up against the wall, their legs spread, their faces pressed against the sandpaper brick.

Hundreds of others stroll past without a hitch, ever. Most of these men walking by are white. This is racial profiling. Here is where racial profiling begins. Prison is the mecca, the birthplace.

This facility employs more than three-hundred-fifty as security and civilian staff. Out of these three-hundred-fifty, I've seen one person of a minority background. He was a middle-aged black officer, who gave the noticeable impression that he hated the job.

On the flip side, the inmate population is overwhelmingly made up of minorities. Nearly three-quarters of the general inmate population is African-American or Hispanic. These two groups account for little more than a third of the country's general population. The over-representation in prison is stunning.

I return from my two-hour workout before the 4:30 p.m. count. Officer Ramsey is back from his two-day hiatus. He's more commonly referred to on the unit as Ram-Rod, The Raminator, or just Douchebag. He's not popular among the inmates, because he's strictly by the book. This guy is a walking manual on Department of Corrections protocol. When he writes tickets, he doesn't consult the rule-book, like other officers do. He doesn't need to. He has the book memorized.

Disobeying a direct order? Tier II, 106.10.

Out of place? Tier II, 102.30.

Disrespecting an officer? Yeah, hold on. Let me call the sergeant. Probably going to be a 112.10, and you'll have thirty days in solitary confinement to mull over whether it was worth calling me a douchebag to my face.

He'll tell me I'm on the dormitory cleanup, as if I'd forgotten what my job has been for the past ten months.

I'll tell him that I know.

I make my protein shake, wash up, and grab my porter weapons. I'm going to tackle the dorm. I follow the same routine, every day: Sweep. Mop. Dust the sills in the dorm area.

I tolerate the same comments from fellow inmates, as I sweep past their cubes.

"Good job. Ram-Rod must be back. Nice technique."

Now and then, I encounter the stray comedian who throws trash into the aisle, just before I pass with the broom.

I try to finish this work as quickly as I can. After all, I'm getting paid seventeen cents an hour. No, that's not a typo. Seventeen cents.

I give the state what they pay me for, as required. Nothing more, nothing less.

When Ramsey's absent, I subcontract my detail out. An over-supply of willing independent contractors exists here, and I place a high opportunity cost on my time. If I can remain in the "office" writing—undisturbed by the menial calling of the State—I will, every time.

"Attention in the compound. Softball game in the yard tonight, followed by the basketball championship between F-Dorm and A-Dorm. Release your one and two sides out to recreation."

I wish they would turn the loudspeaker down. The volume's way too loud. The raucous dorm empties from sixty to ten, just like that.

I head straight back to the "office." I take advantage of the next couple of hours, while the place is actually quiet. I pick up where I've left off.

"Attention in the compound. Open your doors for the recreation exchange."

I lose track of time, immersed in my writing or reading, or whatever it is I'm doing. I quickly grab anything of value and rush back to my cube. I throw my valuables into the locker, change, and grab my book. I lock the locker, and dash out the door just as they announce, "Secure your doors. Recreation run is complete."

I've cut the time close again.

I get pulled over at the gate to the yard by Officer Smitty. He's back from vacation. Smitty is one of the most racist officers in this compound, but it's not overt. If you're white, you're good with him. There's never a problem. He'll pull you aside and talk with you, almost like you're not a convict.

"You decided to show up for work, huh?" he says with a slight grin, intimating he might have unearthed my recent gambit.

While Smitty was on vacation, I, too, was on vacation. For the past week-and-a-half, I have been paying someone a stamp (forty-four cents) to sit out in the recreation shack for my shift, from 8:30 until 10p.m.

The State pays me fifty-one cents for the shift, so I make a robust profit of seven-cents a shift. The real reason

I outsource my time, though, is so I can stay in the "office" uninterrupted, while the majority of the dorm is outside.

The dorm is quiet now. Almost halcyon.

"What do you mean, Smitty? I've been here," I reply.

"My foot, you have. Don't lie to me. I have eyes and ears everywhere in this place," he says. His smile turns to a frown.

I know I've been caught. I'd better tell him the truth. He obviously knows. The guy does have informants all over the compound.

"Okay. I had an arrangement with a friend who said he'd cover the shack for me for the last week or so. I've been real busy with—"

Before I finish, he puts up his hand. "Shhhh…I don't wanna hear your little story. In fact, I don't really give a dang who mans that dumb-ass shack anyhow, as long as someone is in there. Just let me know next time you want to do something like that, and don't make a habit out of it," he says. His frown turns to a slight grin. He motions me back into the stream of inmates, funneling through the tiny gate to the yard.

I say no more, make my way into the current, and disappear.

The shack job's the same every night. I hand out a few belts, a few balls, maybe a paddle. Then I just sit, in the shack or outside on the pail, and read.

Sometimes, I read a book and sometimes, the paper. Maybe, I complete a crossword.

The shack shift lasts for only an hour-and-a-half.

I talk to a few acquaintances. Maybe, I do a loop around the yard, if the cop's cool. Then, it's over. My shift and the day.

I think about the day, the week, the year, my life. The stars are bright, the air crisp. The season has changed.

I think of my family, my parents, my brother. I am filled with love and hope at the thought of them, every time.

I think of my friends and the support they provide, too.

I think of how fortunate I am to have family and friends in my life. Many in here have neither. Many have grown up in this world alone and are forced to fend for themselves. They survive any way they can.

This thought makes me sad. I persevere, though. I must be strong. I must continue to grow and to learn, to soak up life. I must continue helping those I can, those who want the help.

I'm okay. Life is okay. I'm tired, and tomorrow is another day.

*Mark Dennis Smith*

## UNTITLED

i.
Everything is from God.
God is in Heaven. So we are
from Heaven.

ii.
Where we are going is where
we have been already.

Life has no timeline.
It uncurls on the surface of a stretching sphere
and when our flesh is done, we drop
what our souls picked up
at the place where we started out.

*Frank Cavano*

# I AM

i am the ant you stepped on
the foot upon your neck
the infant searching nipple
an old man's "what the heck"
the trembler in the corner
the king with scepter bold
the man collecting bottles
another hoarding gold.
    i am the priest with fetish
    for altar boys so tender
    the self-righteous preacher
    the drunkard on a bender
    the arrogance of the teacher
    the simple wisdom of a child
    the women selling sexy
    young girls by men defiled.
i am the black man's minor chord
in a white man's orchestration
the gay man's thirst for rights
midst biblical condemnation
a politico's self-serving vote
a soldier's fight for democracy.
i am all these polar things but
    none of these are Me.

*Frank Cavano*

# COME

Reprise. Still another day on
hands and knees asking, again
asking. Today I want You, want
Your intervention. What's it this
time? A sickness, worry about a
family member, a loss through
death? Perhaps a repeated error
made for a ten thousandth time
because I wanted to. And then
felt guilty.

Back. Oh, yes I'm back now in
bad times. In good, You were a
luxury I could not afford. You
were too consistent, too placid.
My tiny mind craves drama and
excitement apart from the steady
hand. But now I reach for it again.
Yes, trembling, I reach again for
You. And all I hear You say is
"come."

*Monika John*

# I AM

I am wrapped
in red linen
awaiting the fire.

The pyre is lit.
The flames are ablaze,
the wood piled high.

Bones remain.
The flesh turns to ashes,
my loved ones are watching.

The water takes
what is left of me,
and I am here.

I am observing.

*This poem was written at Pashupatinath Temple, Nepal.*

*Monika John*

## VARANASI

The city dweller's squalor
is your bane,
the pilgrim's quest,
your hope for the future.

The policeman's graft
and the small man's fears
cry to heaven for solution,

while injustice rules
in dusty streets.
Justice is not but by higher laws.

Terror of life and devotion to gods
walk hand in hand,
like siblings
from different fathers.

*Monika John*

## BEGGAR OF VARANASI

She receives the coin
with a humble bow
yet the wave of her hand says
*we are parting as equals, as friends.*

And no one has taken,
and no one has given.
The gentle dignity of her eyes
follows me into my days.

*Airica Parker*

## WILLINGNESS

I am willing
to acknowledge

my limitations,
to accept

both responsibility
and confusion.

I am willing
to prolong awe,

to extend
unknowing,

this nest
full

of becoming.
I am willing

to be
here,

awake
to these pulses

balancing within
delicate shells.

*Airica Parker*

# FOLLOWING

i.

Chipped cement blocks, white
stones, pebbles, and a few marbles
sit in piles. A wide outer circle
is easy to spot. *The eagle is there*,
she says behind rising tobacco,
the rolled cigarette. *I only smoke here,*
*at this praying place. I cannot see*

*the eagle*, I tell her. She nods.
Puff,

puff, dusty-umber clouds,
weighted water, dry syrup,
puff,

puff. She nods behind her smoke,
this time not at me. After a while,

a while more, we continue to climb.
Torn fabric sails in frayed pastels
on low branches: sweetgum, pine.
The children did that. We climb.

ii.
The body spirals inward.
Umbilical cord, mother;
umbilical cord, grandmother
of grandmothers, all of life—
swirling to a pinnacle shaped
like infinity reaching
to complete its sign.

iii.
Sometimes we drift apart.
She becomes a movement,
a rustle, a gesture up ahead.

When I lose her from sight,
the path she helps wear
stays under my feet.

Rounding a corner,
I come back upon her suddenly,

follow her gaze out to other peaks—
powdered navy,

down to forest—
jasmine,

to a clearing—a circle
around a circle
around an eagle.

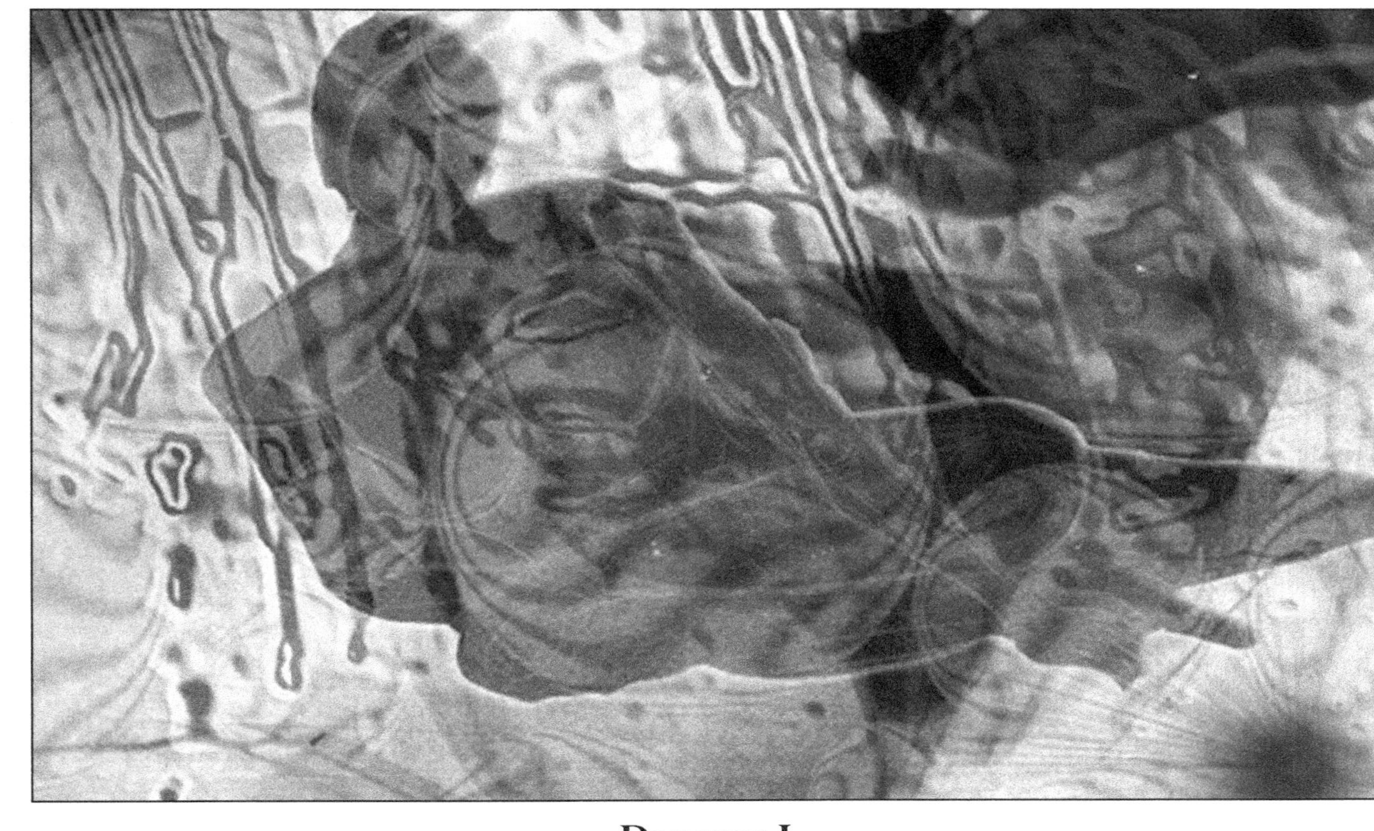

**Dancers I**

Chrystal Berche

**Dancers II**
Chrystal Berche

*T.A. Hunley*

# FOR YOUR VIEWING PLEASURE/ ~~NAKED IN FULL VIEW~~

A pensive night like tonight destroys what little forced tranquility is left inside of you. You're attempting not to hear—to keep distant—the songs of Arcade Fire blaring from the noise box. You're attempting not to absorb in the pith of your being the charging beats, digitized melodies, and subtle reverberations of life-sounds, which force you to acknowledge that the earth stops spinning for no spirit wrapped in flesh, no matter how bruised or violently tattered that spirit may be.

You rest your bleary eyes on the dim and glowing white candle of the Sagrado Corazón de Jesus. The candle burns behind you, never in front, full view—You couldn't stand the shame of seeing the light directly and its directly seeing you, you in all your wretched nakedness reflected in the cigarette-smoke-stained window. You think about glass and how things shatter. ~~And you wonder if the gentle, innocent flame means less since you're not one of the sanctified. The window is filthy with the muck of your lung-killing sin. Smoking transubstantially becomes the sin the man-monster forced onto and into your body, on so many nightmarish childhood nights.~~

You read. You're stuck on/in a sentence that you abashedly fragmented, because that's how your mind copes—You rip out only what matters and leave the rest behind. You think, if you dare call feeling "thinking" in a world where ration and logic too often trump intuition, that the whole world, if it looked through your grime-covered window in this moment, would see you as you are, *might* think the soot was part of your body, and maybe it is, and that you would have nothing to seal your filthy self up in.

The window becomes nothing, a no-thing that is merely part of the action of viewing. You think—Windows don't actually exist, if there is no viewer. You shudder at the cold, matter-of-fact reasoning that your feeling has been sliced into. So flippant. So easy. ~~You think fleetingly of a broken piece of glass sliding under your nails, and you know it's not as painful as the act of remembering what you're trying to ignore tonight.~~

Somewhere, not here (because you're not strong enough to acknowledge that "here" is exactly where the action is happening), the girl in this story—no, you're a woman now—no, you're a girl—is lost. Somebody is trying to find her/you.

Somebody else is looking at you through glass that has become a container for viewing tonight, so that looking in becomes voyeuristically pleasurable, all at your own naked expense. But you know it's impossible for you to be found. Not even the great teachers can get to you. Not even the holy ones whose job it is to get through to you, a single sacred heart, ~~and save you from, what else, yourself, that has been violently soldered to that man forever, through his act of permissionless, sexual ravaging~~.

You're far gone now in the window reflection of the Sagrado Corazón. Somewhere, off in the distance, somebody has the nerve to sing about missionaries—righteous workers that save and shatter, redeem and destroy. ~~You know which~~

~~words are closest to truth, just like you did after those hive laborers tried, and failed, to fix you—all men claiming that God is good, like a grandfather whose knee we sit upon and love. What they didn't know is that a grandfather's lap is only safe in the daylight, never at night when the lights go out.~~

Somewhere, you think there should be a place where people go to wait 'til it's over. "It" is a vague word. That's why you like it. "It" hides things.

But you can't find that place, ~~although you fleetingly glimpsed it once while attempting—and failing—to escape from the predatory beast who tracked your scent no matter which bedroom you asked your grandmother's permission to stay in, while spending the night for many a babysitting sleepover. "Shhhh…don't tell Papaw, Mamaw," you'd say innocently, like it was a game. Underneath your little girl pajamas, your body was beginning to tense and stiffen, and you were mentally separating yourself from it, preparing for what was inescapable once he inevitably found you.~~

~~If you could find such a place, you'd make a reservation to wait to be saved. You'd wait until you found what it is that would heal this silent anguish that screams louder than any real voice ever could or should.~~ Your thoughts fragment further, and you wonder if that place would have glass windows.

A friend once said the only books he rips up for collage are those bountiful-of-copy. Your mind recklessly paraphrases into everyday life to rip out what matters and leave the rest behind. ~~Justice should be served even for those whose bodies are violated in ways not unique, although you don't know what could be just for a crime like this (and the story is all stories).~~

You can't help but think of Nazis and what they did to books and precious bodies, so many destroyed. The ashes are identical—bountiful-of-copy.

Somewhere, you're being ripped apart. You're falling to the ground like shards of glass or paper shreds or ashes. ~~(When glass or books or bodies are destroyed, they become utter non-functioning garbage, no matter how much time has passed since the undoing. You feel this.)~~ Not even the music and the reflection of the candle's sacred heart can reach you.

Now, there's some Nazi rolling glibly in his grave and laughing, because evil still exists. ~~It all inevitably looks the same, you think—Defiled innocence has the same "portrait smile" everywhere, because if the pain surfaced it would destroy everything in its path.~~

~~The one thing a little girl doesn't want to do is destroy someone she loves purely and simply. Some people might say that she shouldn't have loved him at all, but she couldn't help it. In the daytime he was a fun and giving grandfather. He taught her to read, and to love books and stories and make-believe. He took her wherever he went, as his shadow and sidekick and buddy. He bought her orange sherbet push-ups at the corner store, whenever she asked. He could bring forth her gushing giggles with his tall tales and innocent shenanigans, so that she would forget the night-time even existed~~.

You can't help but cringe at the thought of him, because he violated something you needed to love and now can't. Precious words once alive have been silenced.

Words equal life. This you know from your sacred, mother-nurtured beginnings: God spoke, and existence was, is, and will be.

To obliterate words, to silence speech, is utter and final death. Of course, this is not really about the books destroyed, ~~but it is to you, because it can't be about the thing it's actually about. You shamefully realize maybe you're not different after all, because you'd rather be silent than speak about this vile thing that happened to you, because it hurts to talk about, worse than sliding your tongue along the razor sharp edge of a shard of glass~~.

Sometimes, pain is too much. We dance to jungle music with stomping feet for salvation, because we can't scream and wail and gnash our teeth loud enough for anyone who can do anything about it to hear us.

If we were dancing in a box made of glass that held fog from the heat of the sweat of our feet and armpits, we would shatter the box and use the shards to break through to the blood that we need to save us.

Arcade Fire has done it to you tonight, ~~though it could have been any other sound that sounded like your own tortured heart, pounding relentlessly in your ears while he was stole and desecrated your four and then five and then six and then seven and then eight and then nine and then ten year old body until, mercifully through the salvation of nature's growth and maturity, your eleven year old body finally had a mouth and a heart and a mind that was brave enough and strong enough to say no to the grandfather you loved in the daytime~~.

You remember the once upon a time of fairy tales where the good are good and the bad are utterly destroyed, where everything is black-and-white, flippant and easy, when you were free enough to be as free as the Arcade Fire musicians.

~~This was in the once upon a time before the silence of the violation that destroyed you.~~ You could rip up/out your own heart for others, ~~because even little girls know that the cuts gleaned from trampling through thorny brush to pick wild flowers in May for their mothers is a price gladly paid to elicit a single, safe, nurturing hug of warm, tender, and unconditionally forever love.~~ The Arcade Fire musicians know this and so does your friend who rips books. Nothing was evil then, because everything was good.

You feel the difference. You don't give a damn if nobody else senses the change, because the pain is about nobody but you tonight.

Everything good stopped. Silence eventually destroys life utterly and completely, never somewhat and partially with a rhythm or melody still lurking somewhere in the darkness. Everything is lost in silence.

You're not living happily ever after, after all.

The reflection of the Sagrado Corazón in the window has done it to you tonight, ~~though it could have been any other image that reminds you of what your broken container can, for years and years and years now, no longer hold: something pure and clean and holy.~~ Be sure of that. The candle looks like what your heart sounds like—silence that burns everything good, right, and noble in its path, when you don't mean for it to.

The window captures its image nonetheless.

You think that even your thoughts can no longer be trusted.

~~This frightens you, because the thoughts you felt were all you had left, when everything else got ripped out of you. Years after the bodily violence was over, Papaw went to his sweet oblivion of death twelve years ago, without you ever having told him that your grown-up self remembers what he did and that it wasn't okay, without you ever asking—how could he do it and why did he do it to his only granddaughter, who knows he loved her nonetheless~~.

Too much is slipping away now. You desperately squint your eyes, or maybe you surrender in exhaustion and close them altogether. You sit in prayer and gaze at the windowed muck. It is the one thing you can/will believe in, because it exists as much within you as without you—the cigarette smoke residue clinging to the glass:

And the bountiful-of-copy flecks
on the invisible container
mercifully
graciously
rise up
and off
of the glass
and become a
million
shining
points
of
light.

~~The points of light are the eyes of every other girl and woman, and your own mother who loved you warmly, tenderly, and unconditionally forever, every female who was ever violated and can't speak about it out loud, but only in whispers behind windows, because the pain of memories is as violently destructive as the thing itself and hits you when you least expect it,~~

~~like when you're listening to Arcade Fire~~
~~or looking at a candle flame~~
~~or thinking about books or Nazis or glass~~
~~or having feelings that are thoughts.~~
~~And you're drawn,~~
~~you're drawn to the light. You can't look away,~~
~~because the eyes are smiling~~
~~with real smiles shining from gentle hearts that feel~~
~~and understand~~
~~that your vessel is broken,~~
~~they tell you this in one tempered voice:~~
~~It is only in our breaking~~
~~that we fully see what is inside~~
~~what is real~~
~~what is true~~
~~what is strong~~
~~what is good~~
~~what can never be taken, stolen, or ripped out~~
~~even when we're afraid it might on nights like tonight.~~
~~You,~~
~~the beautiful broken you that is you,~~
are

~~still~~
~~here,~~
~~and that~~
~~is~~
~~enough.~~
~~You can't help but~~
~~smile~~
~~the real smile~~
~~with your eyes~~
~~longingly and knowingly looking back.~~
And the pain transubstantiates through the Sacred Mystery
of it all.
And you embrace
the muck.
And you suck in
the muck.
And you love utterly and deeply and fully
the muck.

For this one holy night, you stop feeling and thinking what you've been feeling and thinking about the shame and filth of yourself, and it's because of the muck and everything else, like the howling music of Arcade Fire, and destruction that makes something new despite the Nazis.

The fire from the sacred heart brings light to what stays hidden and never was ugly, although you thought it was, yet no longer care to remember why. You forget that there was ever a window at all, because the glass dissolves when you quit looking at, out, and through it. It is gone, and you are with the world.

Quietly.

You dance to the pulsing beat of the flame. You remember that there's a story somewhere about a girl—no, you're a woman now—no, you're a girl—who is trapped in a box of glass and can't seem to break out. You see the dancing girl through the glass that is a no-thing for viewing. You scream with everything inside of you to the girl in the glass.

You scream to her to break the glass—Break the glass—It isn't really there. For your salvation, girl, break the glass.

The girl, in her dancing fog of tears and sweat, the girl lost in the music of Arcade Fire and fire and fire—stops. She realizes that windows are for viewing, not containing. Finally, she understands.

She screams from the pit of her raging gut with the power of destruction and creation inside of her. The silent power of the scream shatters the box that was never for viewing or containing in the first place. Ashes and empty words bountiful-of-copy fall from her mouth, as she runs through invisible shards of glass that pierce her naked feet.

She runs. She runs. She runs. Blood flows. It flows, and it flows. Her blood from inside her body covers her and every other person that has ever hid because evil had found them.

She, in the fury of her own free-screaming flame, is no longer ashamed. She is no longer afraid. The light of herself, the pure and the clean, obliterates the dark of the night.

The shards of glass disappear. Finally, she finally dances to the music without pain. She is free and beautiful for the whole world to witness:

And the girl is the woman
and the woman is the girl
and you are the woman
and you are the girl
and you are every other woman and girl who ever suffers,
like me,
who gets trapped in a box made of glass
and thinks your muck
is ugly
and are ashamed
and frightened
and silent.

No more.

*Michael Findlay*

## BIRDSONG

*For Li Ho (791-817)*

Gently tugging the jade clasp
she wakes,
her hair spread flat
black on the ivory pillow.

Slender neck craned
to glimpse the morning mist and mottled cloud,
she reaches for her sea green
satin robe.

In the oval mirror
a hand touches her face.
Blood red fingernails
slowly trace eyebrow, cheek,
and chin.
Her brown eyes lock, wary.

Far-off, a murmur.
Footsteps scurry.

The window again.
Pond edge, pearl sky. An egret flaps
and rises on the slight breeze

Silk belt loosely tied,
she sighs, braces for the cold,
lifts the door latch,
and descends steep wood steps
slick with dropped blossom.

Steadying hand on a bough,
she glides to the tall reeds.

Dew dapples her gold slippers.
A weak sun glistens in the deep water.

*Kelley Jean White*

# MY FAITH IS LIKE THIS BASKET

heartshaped, woven,
just big enough to hold
your stone

but my hand cannot grasp the handle

lord, it's heavy
it pulls me down
it blisters my fingers, burns

the reeds and wicker
turn ash and bone

unraveling

it cannot hold
my unfurling
new
blue
wings

*Kelley Jean White*

# NOTHING

mother that was
broken
hovering kite

milk spilled
in the meadow
the sound of stones

a child's smallest
finger
the glass of
her eyes

the wheel kept
from turning
the river sung dry

the moon in your mirror
the lock on your well

the voice of a dewdrop
the failure of dawn

*Lyn Lifshin*

## I WAS FOUR, IN DOTTED

Swiss summer pajamas,
my face a blotch of
measles in the small
dark room over blue
grapes and rhubarb,
hot stucco cracking.
17 North Seminary.
That July Friday
noon, my mother was
rushed in the gray
blimp of a Chevy
north to where my
sister Joy would be
born two months
early. I wasn't
ready either and
missed my mother's
cool hands, her
bringing me frosty
glasses of pineapple
juice and cherries
with a glass straw
as Nanny lost her
false teeth, flushed
them down the toilet,
then held me so tight

I could smell lavender
and garlic in her
braided hair, held
me as few have,
as if—
not to lose more.

*Lyn Lifshin*

# BUT INSTEAD HAS GONE INTO THE WOODS

A girl goes into the woods
and for what reason
disappears behind branches
and is never heard from again.
We don't really know why.
She could have gone shopping
or had lunch with her mother
but instead has gone into
the woods, alone, without the lover,
and not for leaves or flowers.
It was a clear bright day
very much like today.
It was today. Now you might
imagine I'm that girl.
It seems there are reasons, but
first consider: I don't live
very near those trees, and my
head is already wild with branches.

*Judith Tate O'Brien*

## LOVE IS NOT CONSOLATION

*For Simone Weil*

When Love crosses the rocky
border to light,

she carries flowers of consolation.
Last Sunday at Mass, I watched Ray

hold his unresponsive
wife's hand and tuck the Nursing Home blanket

around her shoulders, around her sunken
breasts, while she dreamed whatever dreams Alzheimer's

provides, he reflected on their life's long
rosary of joys. Sorrowful

mysteries, too.
At Communion time Ray bent to rouse her. He stroked

her face—long, slow, soft strokes, like the blue butterfly
I saw last fall fanning patient wings

over a late sun-centered daisy.

*Judith Tate O'Brien*

# BEHOLD

The woman's body knew before the doctors told her—
This first baby would also be her last.

Celeste arrived squalling, almost ugly.
She played with cousins in the backyard dirt.
Her hair grew in thin and temporary.
Her vision dimmed and went out.
She read her last book in high school: *Silas Marner*.

Then, Will came sloshing through
the mud of the mother's crushed dreams
wanting
to marry Celeste.

The mother ordered Chantilly lace
for her daughter's gown,
and said, "Stand up straight."
When Will beheld Celeste
coming to him down the aisle,
his heart broke
into song.

In the dining room
sixty-some years later,
Will introduces her
with a wide arc of arm,
as if holding back a curtain.
“My wife,” he says,
beaming
as if he were saying,
“Behold!”

*Jacqueline Jules*

## INSTRUCTIONS FOR A PANIC ATTACK

Shut your eyes
and inhale
'til you see
a small plastic bottle,
bright blue in color
sitting among the dirty pots
and piles of paper
on your cluttered counter.
Pick it up.
Unscrew the lid.
Dip two shaking fingers
into the soapy water
and retrieve a thin blue wand
with a circle on one end.
Lift it to your trembling lips
and blow
'til a lopsided sphere
hovers in the air
like a hungry mosquito.
Don't wait for it to bite.
Fill your lungs. Exhale. Repeat
'til the bubbles in your chest
drift out the window
and down the street.
They would be smoke rings
in a black and white cartoon.

*Patricia George*

# A DIFFERENT WORLD

Shock to the system
Knock on my window
Badge in my face
Nowhere to hide—
I was fine until you worried about me.

*Patricia George*

## STEADFAST

The world does not understand
your joy in crisis.

Keep it anyway.

**Berlin in the 1920s**

Allen Forrest

*Jamie Donohoe*

# DIVINING SASHA

*Sasha is a precocious 15-year-old. She is speaking to somebody or something she trusts that can't talk back, perhaps a stuffed animal she's retained from childhood, or a photograph of one of her heroes—Gloria Steinem and Marina Abramovic.*

**Sasha:** At lunch, you can either hide away in the library or hole up in some lonely teacher's classroom OR you can try the quad where the *obbligato* giggling of high school Kardashians is incessant, while sophomore and junior boys gape and bark like dogs through the glossy halls of freshman meat. But no matter how hard you try to remain on the fringes of this hormonal pool, some guy will always check you out, because you have boobs. (Beat) It's so weird, that moment when you're talking to some guy and his eyes slip. Then he glances up and sees you're looking at him, and it's clear you know he was just looking at your boobs, and he knows you know he was looking at your boobs—and you're supposed to just carry on and pretend that you're both truly interested in Holden Caulfield or Game of Thrones or whatever you were just talking about. All this bizarre sub-text is starting to happen, and I have to think on multiple levels about what kind of necklace I wear. What is that? These days, a crucifix isn't a symbol of faith. It's a boob magnet, a nubile divining rod. Either you drape yourself in sweatshirts thick as bullet proof vests or you're serving your goods up on a platter, and you have to deal with it because that's the way it is. It's so weird, having your body be this thing which is totally out of control, which will be read in all these ways by complete strangers. Intellectually, I get that a woman is both imprisoned and empowered by her body, that a woman is objectified by men but that she can also use her body to get what she wants. What do I want? What do I want that I need to wriggle my chest to get? I just want to study, get the heck out of here, go to an Ivy League school and then…I don't know. (Beat) I mean, I want to be included. I don't want to be some Hester Prynne who doesn't get asked to senior ball because of her puritanical snobbiness. And I do get crushes on guys. Well, guy. Pierce Fullerton, who doesn't know I exist because I'm in all AP classes, mostly, and he's not. He's two years older, and his girlfriend looks like a 25-year-old pole-dancer. (Beat) I wish I was a lesbian.

*Gabriele Zuokaite*

## MORNING

I woke up.
It was the same morning.
He was still in my bed.
I wanted him out.
He was snoring.
I didn't enjoy what I saw.
He was no more hot or sexy.
He looked boring.
I was bored.
He woke up.
He expected me to smile.
Fine. I smile. See?
Now get out!
Why are you still here?
I ate lobster last night, alone.
I smile one more time.
Stop, don't touch me there.
This is my private square.

He loved me, but I don't care.

*Stuart Friebert*

# BANDUDELUMING

i.

Everybody was looking forward to Schnooty Grunzer's solo flight in mid-October.

Schnooty was Augie Hahn's best friend by far, and practically moved in with the Hahns after his parents were killed in an auto accident, though Uncle Jerry, his mother's sometimes sober brother, went through the legal hoops to adopt him.

Uncle Jerry mostly slept at the air-field, where he was chief mechanic. He smoothed the way with the flight folks for Schnooty. "Fly now, pay later," he chirped.

"What a beautiful way to celebrate the first anniversary of the end of the war," Augie's mother said of the solo flight, and announced she'd make Schnooty his very own strudel.

Other news on the block was that Harlene Holman was soon to be released from the Detention Home north of Racine. For a moment Scnooty's friend Augie thought he'd try to get to her before Schnooty, if only to make Schnooty jealous.

"I don't care if she makes me wait 'til I'm in a rocker on the nursing home porch. I'll be there at the end to rescue her from her last mess-up," Schnooty once said said, punching Augie's arm and howling.

Augie had sworn to keep Schnooty's secret.

Now, Augie had some cockeyed notion he would borrow his Uncle Max's horse-and-milk wagon, rumble down to Racine, and be there when Harlene stepped into the street.

Uncle Max said, "Fine with me," because Harlene was being released on a Sunday.

Augie couldn't back down. He got up at dawn, made sure he had enough water and some hay for the horse, and managed to show up at the Detention Home by the time Harlene appeared in the doorway.

She stumbled a moment in the bright sunlight, before stepping out to start up her problematic life again.

In his naive way, Augie thought she'd be happy to have a funky if slow ride back to South Milwaukee. He had Uncle Max's warmest blanket out on the side seat for her.

Harlene saw him all right—hard to miss a horse-and-dairy wagon on such a small street—but moments later, Benny Pulaski pulled up right behind the wagon in his little roadster, its top rolled down in spite of the chill in the air, and she didn't hesitate.

"Sorry you came all this way, Augie. Really sorry," Harlene said, hopping in beside Benny, who revved the engine and nearly took the back wheel of Uncle Max's wagon off on his swerve onto the road.

"Darn nice of you, Augie. I'm really sorry!" Harlene called out as they shot by.

Schnooty said if he'd been out flying, he'd have buzzed down to scare "the bejesus out of those goldarn fools," but Augie pretended nothing worth going on about had happened.

Something more worrisome was happening in their lives.

ii.

Mrs. Hahn was starting to "stink." She herself announced this openly to everybody's surprise, after one of her signature old-world suppers; she was usually private about personal matters.

At first, she thought the smell might be the trillium tea she'd been consuming to still the sudden shooting pains that sent her to the couch several times a day. The label promised the tea would "kiss your cares away" in no time. When she stopped the remedy for a few days, however, the stink was still in the air.

Augie brought home little perfume samplers from Ray's Pharmacy, where he was in training. He helped himself to these when Mr. Ray wasn't looking.

They didn't mask her odors.

Soon, she seemed to lose some of her usual boundless strength. She resorted to using an old cane Mr. Hahn had inherited from an intrepid Hungarian uncle.

"It got him up and down the Alps, so it should get you around the house, Hermine," Mr. Hahn said to soothe her in his funny way.

Augie, Uncle Max, Uncle Jerry, and Schnooty joined forces and put their foot down.

"You've got to see a doc at the clinic, Auntie," Uncle Max pleaded. "Right now, this week, no more delays. If you won't make an appointment, I will, and I'll take off a day if need be to get you there."

"Uncle Max is right, Ma," Augie chipped in, to the nods of Uncle Jerry and Schnooty. "Besides, we're finding out more and more every day. Lots of new medicines come into the store every week. We see people who're suffering something terrible get some relief. Do it for us. Please, Ma!"

Mr. Hahn sat by and said nothing.

Mrs. Hahn could see he was worried, too; so, she gave in. "All right, all right, but promise me you won't throw my teas out!" She had a way of making you laugh, Augie would say, just when you needed to.

iii.

Uncle Max got kicked by his horse, who'd been spooked by a clanging streetcar, and had to take to bed for a while. Meanwhile, Mr. Ray refused to allow Augie time off to take his mother to the clinic, even though he'd more or less agreed to, earlier.

"Lately, you've been doing too little, Hahn," he'd said. Not selling enough large sizes, putting too many sprinkles on ice cream cones. I could go on, but I'm counting on you to step up your commitment to this enterprise, Hahn."

It was as if a door had banged open on more disasters.

Mr. Hahn was left to take his wife to the clinic, though at times of crisis, he became disoriented.

Augie wrote explicit instructions for which streetcars they should take to reach the West Side, just north of Downtown. He rehearsed the route with his father.

His mother said she'd try to stay alert at the transfer station, where several lines crossed. Augie realized she couldn't be depended on, either.

Desperate, he decided to ask the old nurse, whom Mr. Ray employed part-time to help the elderly customers with intimate decisions about douchebags, enemas, and the like, if she'd be free to accompany his parents. She happened to be free that day and readily agreed.

She'd actually worked at the clinic years ago. She was understandably curious about the latest medical advances.

"Besides," she added, "who knows. They might want me back."

When he tried to press a few dollars into her hand, she seemed offended.

He just thanked her, instead.

"Nothing beats a genuine 'thank you,' young man," she said, patting his cheek. "No worries now, you hear? If it's comfortable for your parents, I can sit in on the examination and take notes. I know how hard it is to listen and to get things straight, especially when doctors talk so fast. And with their terrible handwriting, sometimes, you can't even read the prescriptions. It's a wonder more folks don't die."

iv.

Mr. Hahn got his hackles up when the old nurse started into the examination room with Mrs. Hahn. Accepting her help negotiating the streetcar journey had been enough.

The nurse told Augie later, much to his chagrin, that his father had actually begun cursing her. He'd turned her toward the waiting room and given her something of a push, as well. It was all she could do, honoring their agreement, to calmly escort them back home.

"How old?" the doctor's nurse asked. "How old is she?" She asked as if Mrs. Hahn weren't there at all, directing her questions to Mr. Hahn.

"She'll be sixty-one in January," he said.

Looking down at her swollen feet, Mrs. Hahn said faintly, “Age never meant that much to me.”

“We’ll take over from here,” the doctor’s nurse said. She then motioned Mr. Hahn back to the waiting room.

He was frankly relieved. He took a seat as far away as possible from the other nurse in his life. He broke off staring at her, when she refused to stop glaring at him.

After a good hour had passed, the doctor came out and sat down gravely at Mr. Hahn’s side. “She’d better be hospitalized right now,” he said. “She’s severely dehydrated. She’s lost quite a few pounds from her normal weight, you know.”

“What did she say?” Mr. Hahn asked, as he looked away, his eyes blurring.

“Well, she’s not too happy, but she didn’t say no. The rest is up to us, my friend.”

Mr. Hahn made an effort to shake the doctor’s hand. He followed the doctor down the hall. His wife had dressed and come out into the waiting room. She was left standing alone, until he caught himself and returned to her side.

Mrs. Hahn made lists of everything that needed to be done while she was in the hospital. She searched out her simplest recipes that the “boys” would be able to follow. She insisted on giving the house a good cleaning before she packed for what the doctor thought might be at most two weeks away.

Mr. Hahn needed watching over. Uncle Max, who lived alone and had pretty well recovered from his accident, offered to take time off from work now and then to check in on him.

This reassured Augie, who was afraid Mr. Ray would fire him if he asked for another personal favor.

"We'll be the five Musketeers," Uncle Jerry said, trying to be jolly.

After they'd each kissed Mrs. Hahn goodbye, Uncle Jerry lined up Mr. Hahn, Augie, Uncle Max, and Schnooty in the hospital corridor. He linked their arms and demonstrated a high, kicking step.

When he tried to add a song to their repertoire, they wound up in different keys.

Strutting past the nurses' station, they bowed, blew kisses, and distributed the little boxes of chocolates Augie bought at a discount from the store. This earned them a round of applause.

v.

Mrs. Hahn asked to go home for a few days, when the cancer broke free of her colon, traveling everywhere at once. Clearly, the end was near.

She'd had to miss Schnooty's solo flight. This saddened her.

Schnooty promised her a ride if she survived.

To everyone's surprise, including her own, she blurted out, "Yes, yes, oh my yes, oh thank you dear boy, yes."

No way was she going to miss bandudeluming either, she added, even if she had to be carried to the side of the park pond when winter's first ice started forming on the surface.

As a young girl in Senice, which she pointed to on Czechoslovakia's page in the atlas, she'd loved to run across thin shore ice. It quaked underfoot.

"If you were lucky, it bent but didn't break," she'd say, locking her green eyes on you.

Once, when Augie was a baby, she'd taken him for a winter outing in the park. There, she came across a bunch of kids daring the ice just as she had back in Senice.

She had half a mind to join them, calling out in jest, "And just what do you think you're doing, you naughty children?"

"We're bandudeluming." a little girl shouted back, her cheeks ripe as a cherries. "That's what we're doing, lady."

From that moment on, Hermine Hahn had rediscovered her only real sport, she'd say.

She summoned up her last reserves when Augie, Uncle Max, Uncle Jerry, and Schnooty came to take her to watch the children try the season's first ice, to see if it would bend, not break.

Mr. Hahn had gone ahead in the park with a bundle of blankets he pulled on Augie's old sled. He found two empty benches to camp on. He marched up and down, flapped his arms, and beat one mitten into the other, to stay warm while he waited.

Finally, a wheelchair appeared on the crest of the hill above the pond. He had to look twice to see that his wife was in it. She sat bundled up, so that just her forehead and eyes were visible.

Uncle Max hollered down, "Tried it yet?"

"Bandudeluming is reserved for my darling wife," he said. He kissed her forehead, when she rolled to a stop at his side.

Her eyes lit up, when Augie offered to run off for roasted chestnuts.

She managed to nibble on a chestnut, her eyes drifting to the children who edged out onto the ice. Her hand lifted for a tiny wave.

One little girl waved back.

"God bless," Mrs. Hahn whispered. Then she turned with effort and said to all of them, who stood there as if at attention, "Let's go bandudeluming."

Mr. Hahn began to cry, softly.  Uncle Max, Augie, Schnooty, and Uncle Jerry almost joined in.

"Sure, Ma. Sure thing," Augie choked out, "but you've got to do your part. Beat this thing. Then, we will. Oh, we will."

"Will what?" she suddenly said, more lost than ever. "Will what, will what?"  Her desperation piled up like shore ice in the coldest weather.

"Will make it home by dark, my love,"  Mr. Hahn said through sobs. "And not get spanked."

vi.

For the service at the funeral home, the five musketeers locked arms in the front row—Mr. Hahn between Augie and Uncle Max, Schnooty next to Augie, and Uncle Jerry on the other side of Uncle Max. The rabbi led the gathering in prayer and began his remarks.

Mr. Hahn soon became restless. He grew even more so, when the rabbi mixed up the facts about Mrs. Hahn's life, which the family had carefully fed him. Finally, Mr. Hahn lost all composure. He sat bawling like a hysterical child.

When the rabbi closed on a prayer for poor Erna's soul, Mr. Hahn shouted out, "Her name is Hermine, not Erna. Damn you. At least get that straight."

The rabbi did not hang around for refreshments.

After the food was eaten, the drinks drunk, and almost everyone gone, Schnooty offered to fly Mr. Hahn, Augie, and Uncle Max over the grave. He would waggle his wings.

Uncle Jerry quashed the idea: "You'd lose your license, and I'd lose my job, kid."

Mr. Hahn hugged Schnooty for the beauty of the idea. Then, he headed for his bedroom.

Schnooty made for the cot on the porch, while Uncle Jerry and Uncle Max said they'd see if the bar around the corner was still open for a final tribute.

Augie sank into his father's old easy chair and stretched his feet out on the hassock. He pulled down over his eyes the intricately beautiful antimacassar, which his mother had crocheted as a young seamstress back in Senice. He finally dozed off, only to wake with a chill, thinking he heard a noise.

He looked in at Schnooty on the porch.

Schnooty was peacefully sleeping, also beneath an afghan Mrs. Hahn had made.

Then, the noise started up again: a thump, thump, thump from above. *The attic. Check the attic*, he commanded himself and took the stairs two at a time.

vii.

His father stood at the little rose window, his old woolen cap pulled down over his ears. He was tapping a cocked pistol against the sill.

Augie knew his father owned a rusty twelve-gauge shotgun, but had never seen the pistol before. He froze.

Finally, Mr. Hahn said, "I'm wondering if it's better to kill something flying by outside. Any ideas?"

Augie broke through his fear. In an instant, he wrapped his arms around his father from behind, knocking the pistol from his hand. It clattered to the floor and went off.

The bullet grazed an old picture of Mr. Hahn's mother. It had been hanging by a thread in the attic for years, because no one wanted to see her grim countenance on a daily basis. The picture crashed to the floor, and the frame broke.

The crash of the picture and the crack of the pistol's report would have awakened the dead. Schnooty said as much, after everyone came running.

Together, they carted Mr. Hahn off to the bed he'd shared with Mrs. Hahn.

"For forty years. Think of that," Mr. Hahn kept saying, when they tucked him in.

Augie put his finger to his lips and gently pulled the covers up around his chin.

*Margreta von Pein*

# THE END

Another chunk of time, lost. It's like I don't want to be alive anymore. I'm done. The snow falls, muffling the cabin. The stove fire is banked and damped down for the night. Rob did that. I'll be warm. Then, I'll die.

Rob will come by with food, which I won't eat. Maybe, he'll have a joke for me. Then, he'll go away again.

"Not to disturb you," he'll say.

Maybe, he won't be able to come up the hill again in the morning. Maybe, he'll be tired himself and stay in bed in his cabin, and when he makes it up in a day or two, I'll be gone. He'll look through the dim glass, brush the snow away, and find me in this bed, peacefully asleep, forever. He'll know, then.

Today, I'm alive and look like I want to be alone. Tomorrow, I'll look cold and stiff and will have achieved forever, alone.

Why do I play this end game?

Rob hikes up, brings in a gust of cold snowy wind, and refreshes the cabin air. He scatters snow about, as he takes off his parka and boots.

He puts the pan of water on the stove. He continues to take his clothes off down to his long johns and crawls under the blanket next to me. We hug each other, rubbing our bodies together. He lies close to me, warming up.

"I'm leaving," I say. Eyes shut, legs straight out, I'm lying on my back with my arms at my side.

He takes my hand.

"When?"

"Soon."

"Why? You don't have to go on my account. I like you here and me down there," he says, meaning his new cabin by the river.

What can I say to him? He's my big brother, my uncle, my sometimes-lover, and my best friend. I've known him from the beginning. He's been through it all with me and never doubted.

He laughs only a little at my arrogance.

"It's about time. Nothing left to do," I say.

"Okay. Can I stay the night?"

I look at him, and he knows the answer is no. He knows I am speaking in metaphor.

He gets out of bed, exchanging his warmth for a rush of cold air. He taps old coffee grounds into the pan on the stove. He goes into the storage room and rummages around. I watch but can't see in the gloom what he is doing.

He comes out with the old rawhide snow shoes.

"I'll leave the good ones in case you need to get out," he says, meaning to the outhouse. "I can use these down below. The snow's not deep yet."

Through the dim window glass, the snow wavers like a thick gray curtain.

He puts on his long-sleeved, button-up undershirt and sits on the bed. He looks at me.

We are old.

His eyes are tiny, surrounded by wrinkles.

I see only a sliver of his ice blue crescents. His nose is puffy, fat, and distorted, the way noses get from a lifetime of drinking. When he smiles, his lips crack; he habitually passes his tongue tip over them, top and bottom. A few white tufts of hair stick out, some around his ears and one in the middle of his crown. From the corners of his eyes, lines radiate in evenly spaced concentric half-circles, all the way to his hairline.

He squints to see me. He only wears glasses to read.

I wear glasses all the time. I can't see anything without them.

I can't hear either. I'm deaf and no longer wear the hardware to help me. I figure I can speech-read all I need to know. I don't need to listen to language anymore.

My hair is white and long and probably a matted mess. I don't care. Two vertical frown lines mark the inner ends of my eyebrows. I never regularly wore sunglasses until I was 70. I squinted into the sun.

Rob's square, scarred hands rest on the blanket. He holds a piece of it between his thumb and forefinger. He is the last person I will see before I die. It's a nice vision to go out with.

The pan on the stove rocks rhythmically from side to side, accompanying the boiling water inside. I have nothing to say.

Rob moves the pan to the back of the stove. Its rocking stops. He takes two slices of bread from their tin and tosses them onto the stove-top to warm. "Cheese?"

I shake my head. I'm not eating, anymore. I hardly drink anything.

"A little water," I say.

He turns the warming bread over, dips a cup into the coffee water, and brings it to me. The water's hot and tastes pale.

He peels two slices of cheese off the stack in the tin and places them precisely on the toast. "Sure?" he asks again.

I nod, yes.

Now, I wish he'd leave me. I want to sleep.

*I feel a spark inside me.*

I can nod off while he's here. He'll leave when he wants.

"You feel sick?" he asks.

"No. Tired. But I'm okay."

*I feel the spark of cosmic fire, the fire that burns toward God.*

*Bonnie Stanard*

# JOURNALING FAITH

A pickup truck carrying a load of crosses in the back
gave me a ride and a place to stay,
but there were splinters in the flatbed
and little suckers that took my blood.

I heard from my many friends
that if you repeat what God says
nightmares won't grow in your back yard.
Pretending is something I learned
to do with my lips.

It doesn't seem appropriate to think of birth as defeat,
but uninvited stones
stand in the church yard.
Strange harmony sounds between the ears
when we no longer see as defeat
the bloody delivery of goodbye
in the sack of birth.

I measure my faith against previous impurities
to find my heritage:
buried people who were blessed
with their own doubts, blinding musts, and needy beliefs.
Many a time they stood outside the church
and listened to the singing.

With the passage of the present,
I am persuaded
by all that's green and mumbles
that nobody knows why we say goodbye.
Still, there's a skill in scribbling notes
on comment cards for future generations.

*Bonnie Stanard*

# NATURAL PIETY

## i. The Last Décor, Supper Table

At my mother's church
an oak tree with a toehold in the cemetery
honors the earth in October.
Acorns fall so brown they shroud the ground
like a ratty burlap sack.
It's impossible to cross the yard
without picking up a handful for your pocket
to take home and make into a wreath,
some such arrangement as will benefit
and decorate a brown table.
There, as many as twelve
can sit with wine and bread.

It doesn't take a rooster's crowing
to realize: colorful paints, plastic greenery,
and artful influences try to defy the fate of the acorns
foretold three times over.

## ii. When Three Days Are Not Enough

The acorn's flavor is bitter.
It benumbs the lips that dare to taste.

The ground beneath the tree
when besotted with plentiful rains
indulges in bitterness in spite of itself,
not without some expectation
that days will pass,
that when the chill is over
a seedling will arise.

Plain brown and bitterness
aren't obvious miracles.
The season of doubt endures.

*Raul Palma*

# HOLY GHOST

The pope visited West Miami the month Alejandro thought he'd receive his First Communion. Despite the threat of lightning storms, a quarter-of-a-million people were in attendance at Tamiami Park's outdoor exposition center.

Some arrived early, claiming sections of the grass or pavement with beach chairs, picnic blankets, and umbrellas. Others arrived late, having traveled far, overslept, or heard about the visit at the last minute.

Some people felt indebted to God, which was the reason they never arrived at all. Somewhere along the line, they'd asked for a miracle—the health of a premature child, the curing of cancer, the successful crossing of a family member through the Florida Straits—and God had answered their prayers. Now, they felt that they should show their devotion and appreciation. These people did not drive, walk, or run to see the pope. They crawled.

Now and then, people could be seen dragging themselves along the searing pavement and performing the sign of the cross. Reporters were perplexed by this expression of devotion. They would stood by these pilgrims and offered a play-by-play account. Many of the religious zealots arrived at Tamiami Park with their knees and elbows cut with glass to discover that the exposition center was full, their admittance denied.

All along Coral Way and 107th Avenue, vendors sold holy relics. Posters of the pope, authentic rosaries, holy water pulled from the River Jordan. News helicopters circled the park, documenting the masses and the traffic, speculating as to whether or not the pope would address Fidel Castro's ban on Christmas. His was not, however, a political visit.

Alejandro's Sunday school instructor had encouraged all students to attend this momentous occasion. It would be a day that none of the children would forget, a day that would forever sear the love of God onto their souls.

Most of Alejandro's peers attended.

Alejandro didn't, though he lived across the street from the exposition center. He had to help his grandfather clear the mangos from the rain gutters.

⌘

Earlier that summer, Alejandro's grandmother had asked him to tone down talk of religion in the house: "God is important," she said, "but not so important." She'd told him a story about the blessed Imelda, who became so enraptured and elated while taking her communion that she keeled over and died. "You don't want to be like Imelda, do you?"

Alejandro and his grandmother sat out on the lanai on a long swing, watching the afternoon rains knock mangos off the trees. Some mangos rolled out onto the grass up against the yard's concrete wall, but there were others that fell onto the aluminum canopy. Those mangos could clog the rain gutters or worse, rot under the sun and attract pests like flies and ants.

"Imelda's buried in Bologna, you know," his grandmother said, "in Italy, under a wax statue of herself. I've put my ear to her lips. If you listen carefully, you can still hear her soul screaming."

"No, you can't," Alejandro said. "I'm not a kid anymore, Mima. I know that good souls go to heaven and bad souls go to hell, not into statues."

"You don't know it all," she said. She explained that he was right about heaven and hell, though some souls, maybe most souls, are neither good nor bad. Those souls are reincarnated. "Instead of going to heaven, they turn into something else, like a mango or a lizard or a wax statue of Imelda," she concluded.

"Please not a lizard."

"But you can be other things, too: a tree, a quarter, a remote control," she said.

"Or a communion wafer?" Alejandro asked, smiling. He pictured Jesus pulled down from the cross, his body drained and torn and shaped into the holy sacrament.

⌘

Alejandro's grandfather, a thin old man scarred by childhood polio, walked with a limp. On Sundays he stayed home instead of going to Mass. The living room was his chapel. He'd hung around, scratching his hairy chest and watching music videos that he'd recorded on VHS cassette tapes: Michael Jackson, Ricky Martin, Gloria Estefan.

His grandfather was held accountable for only two chores on Sundays. Taking out the garbage and clearing the mangos from the rain gutters. There were many flash storms during mango season, so the gutters would often fill with baby mangos.

Across the street, the pope was speaking.

"Hold the ladder for me," Alejandro's grandfather said, setting its rungs up against the roof.

Alejandro squared up under the ladder and watched his grandfather climb to the top. He pressed his thumbs into the wood grain. The wood in his hands seemed malleable yet sturdy, only creaking when his grandfather twisted back to drop mangos onto the grass. Alejandro wondered whether Jesus had reincarnated into this sort of wood—the kind ladders are made of—him being a carpenter and all.

All the while, Alejandro could hear the pope's prayers, muffled by the crowds from across the street.

⌘

The first stage of Sunday school culminates with a written examination. Children need to prove that they understand the importance of the Holy Communion before they can accept the body and blood of Christ. Class is held in St. Agatha's adoration chapel—a small white room with the night sky painted on its ceiling.

With only four pews, children in Alejandro's class would fight for a good seat. Alejandro, however, did not partake in this struggle. Instead, he would sit in the aisle, with his back against the wall. In avoiding the scuffle, he felt charitable, worthy beneath the stained glass windows.

Alejandro expressed his charity in other ways, too. He held the doors before and after Mass. He participated in the church's bake sales and concerts. Once, he even volunteered to be one of the apostles in an annual reenactment of the Last Supper, a widely attended Mass. This was quite an honor, since he was not yet prepared to receive Communion.

The Last Supper scene was re-enacted with young boys, so Father Lopez offered apple juice in place of wine. When that apple juice spilled onto Alejandro's tongue, he spat it back into the chalice and gagged. His fellow apostles couldn't believe what had happened. They nearly refused the blood of Christ, too.

After Mass, several of the volunteer apostles tracked Alejandro down. With their fake beards and full-length tunics flapping in the wind, they threatened to punch him out.

Alejandro was saved by a downpour. He ran home, fleeing distant lightning strikes.

⌘

On the day of the Communion examination, Alejandro lay flat on the floor of his Sunday school class to fill out the questionnaire. He knew the answers to most of the twenty-five questions.

1. Why did God create you? *To love him.*

2. Who is Jesus? *He is God.*

3. Is Jesus' father God? *Yes.*

But there was one question that stumped him:

18. Who is the Holy Spirit? *The deity responsible for reincarnation*, he answered.

The Sunday school instructor wanted to know where Alejandro had learned about reincarnation. In a parent-teacher conference, the instructor explained to his grandmother that reincarnation is a mystical fantasy. Catholics believe in the Resurrection and in heaven.

Alejandro's grandmother confessed to teaching her grandson about reincarnation, but only because she'd read about it in a magazine.

Finally, Alejandro was allowed to retake his Communion examination under the watchful eye of his instructor.

He passed. Still, he had not been prepared to receive his First Communion in time for the Pope's visit.

⌘

Alejandro stopped volunteering at the church or holding doors. During Sunday school, he fought for a seat in one of the back pews. He began asking his grandmother for permission to skip out on church and Sunday school, so that he could play baseball with the other boys. And when his grandfather one day enlisted Alejandro's help with the ladder, Alejandro rolled his eyes.

The Dade County Youth Fair was in town. At the site of the Tamiami Exposition center, roller coasters and spinning rides had been assembled, seemingly overnight. Alejandro wanted to go to the fair with his friends. He wanted to see what an Elephant Ear was and get sick on the Gravitron or lost in the House of Mirrors.

To the sound of a roller coaster dropping and the screams of its passengers, his grandfather climbed to the top of the ladder.

He twisted back to dump mangos into the grass.

This time, Alejandro was not holding the ladder but meandering through the garden, trying to sneak a peek at the amusements beyond the wall. Then, the ladder tipped, sliding from the rain gutters and falling backwards into the grass.

*Barry W. North*

# IN GOD'S OWN HANDWRITING

*For an eleven-year-old girl,*
*killed in an ATV accident during Thanksgiving week*

*I tell you the truth. Unless you change*
*and become like little children,*
*you will never enter the kingdom of heaven.*

—*Jesus Christ*

Her photo in the obituaries
is as out of place
as sunlight inside a cave.
Everything about her,
from the braces on her teeth
to the smile on her thin face,
made even thinner by the waterfall
hair cascading down on either side,
shouts out: "I do not belong here."
One look at her,
even in black and white,
and you know
she would have been the sun
in any galaxy she chose to inhabit.

Not even Death could
put out her light.

She was up early this morning,
stealing hearts all over the city
with this photo I hold in my hands,
this photo that tries to contain her,
to keep her still.
Her smile springs to life,

as though she has stepped off the page
right into the office
of the school secretary,
as though she waits patiently for her permission slip
to return to her sixth-grade classroom,
to her classmates,
and to the rest of her busy life:
to spirit club meetings,
to the track team
and volleyball practice,
before going back home
to her family,
who could not
envision life without her.

I stare at her photo until my eyes hurt;
still I cannot look away.
I imagine how strange
the everyday life
in that family must be now
like morning without the breath of dawn.

I love this little girl,
who had everything we left behind
in the garden,
in God's own handwriting
written across her face which,
paper-thin,
I am holding in my hands,
telling myself to let it go.

*Scott David*

# THE BATHTUB SHELTER

The bathtub Jesus on the front lawn of Saint Linus Catholic Church in Sabbaday Falls went missing on a brisk February morning just before Mardi Gras. Deputy Sheriff Fulton Braver investigated the disappearance. He was a lusty oversized cop with an expansive scalp, apostate religious views, a peacock swagger, and a passion for his dear mother Mary's mac & cheese with frozen peas. He was delighted by Monsignor O'Brien's spiritual misfortune.

Braver had the Monsignor repeat again and again how he was not precisely sure when the statue had taken flight.

"Between six and ten o'clock on Sunday evening, I estimate," the Monsignor said uncertainly.

"Too much holy wine Sunday night, Monsignor?" Braver joked. "Can't quite recall when Our Lord and Savior hit the road?"

Monsignor O'Brien summoned what was left of the considerable dignity he had possessed, until the expected appointment to the Vatican had failed to come through. Pointedly, he suggested that the deputy begin sifting for clues.

The ensuing investigation produced immediate results. Within an hour, the St. Linus sacristan, Jack Flaherty, surrendered.

Jack had been looking for an excuse to be a martyr ever since World War II. Then, he had been deemed too young for service, and thus in his view, cheated out of his requisite bravery and glory.

Jack confessed to the theft of the Jesus. He insisted that Braver place him behind bars, so that he could suffer for his sins.

Braver would gladly have closed the case, but for the inconvenient witness of the Right Reverend Alice Standish. She pointed out that, at the approximate time of the statue's disappearance, Jack had been on a mad shuffleboard winning streak down at Our Lady of the Ages Nursing Home, which Jack visited from time to time to make himself feel good about his lot in life.

The weight of the evidence was overwhelming. Braver had no choice but to set Jack free.

Jack beelined for the Watchworks Tavern and Grill, got drunk, took off all his clothes, and asked loudly to be swaddled like a child in the manger. His long-suffering wife fetched him and brought him home.

As Fat Tuesday turned into Ash Wednesday, news of the theft spread from one house of prayer to another. Hasty cabals were convened at tables of the Watchworks Tavern, in the aisles of the local True Value, and at the shuffleboard courts of Our Lady of the Ages. The Saint Linus Catholics blamed the Saint James Catholics, and both sets of Catholics blamed an imagined conspiracy of Methodists, Baptists, and atheists. Everyone suspected Tarsy, the town's token gay secular Jew, but Sabbaday Falls relied on Tarsy for the fresh fruit he sold from a portable stand seven days a week, the Sabbath included. The Unitarians had no particular view on the matter, so long as all parties' self-esteem remained intact.

Only the Episcopalians of Druthers Hill—led by the Right Reverend Standish, a Mayflower descendant whose ancestors had founded Sabbaday back in 1648 when Catholics were heathen—were exempt from suspicion. Everyone agreed that bluebloods of their ilk were unlikely to be mixed up in conduct so tawdry for a prize ungilt.

In a burst of ecumenical generosity at the next Sunday's homily, Monsignor O'Brien deemed the Episcopalians to be close enough to Catholics in temperament and ceremony as to be honorary victims of the theft.

The Right Reverend Standish issued a curt statement rejecting this association in its entirety.

Brother Earl Everett, who ran the Sabbaday Savings Bank in his spare time, did not hesitate to capitalize on the situation. That same Sunday, he preached extensively on the price of idolatry and the wages of sin. Brother Earl had assiduously cultivated a reputation for speaking directly with God, though townspeople often noted a strange coincidence between God's demands, Brother Earl's personal wants, and the bottom line of Sabbaday Savings.

After a week without the statue, Monsignor O'Brien summoned Sabbaday's religious leadership to St. Linus for an emergency ecumenical council. Chef Duchaine from the St. Linus Rectory was put to work feeding the assembled leaders.

Chef had lost a step mentally over the years. This mattered little, because he had never been much of an intellectual athlete. He had rounded shoulders and a basset-hound-face. His look was one of such weary curiosity that it seemed he saw everything new again, no matter how many times he had seen it before. The chef was nevertheless an acknowledged culinary genius (second only perhaps to Deputy Braver's mother, Mary).

Using fruit purchased from Gay Tarsy, Chef Duchaine created an out-of-season pear-raspberry cobbler that all the religious in attendance proclaimed to be God's own work.

Brother Earl deigned to attend the ecumenical council meeting, despite grave theological misgivings. He took the prior precaution of enjoying a pre-council meal on the house at the Watchworks Tavern, which was behind on its mortgage payments to Sabbaday Savings. He had developed a strange notion that Father O'Brien dined on holy hosts alone, and didn't want to go hungry at the meeting.

Brother Earl's pitstop at the Watchworks Tavern didn't stop him from accepting three helpings of the cobbler in question upon arriving at the council meeting. His opinion of Catholics was thereby vastly (albeit temporarily) improved.

The council itself didn't share the cobbler's success. Monsignor O'Brien loudly proclaimed that society couldn't last if people were just up and thieving Jesuses. He boldly predicted a rash of snatched statuary and empty pedestals all over town. Few of his fellow clerics, however, shared his sense of urgency. They were more concerned about the council's protocols.

When Monsignor O'Brien attempted to bless the food and the assembly, Gertrude Stein Litovchenko, a Unitarian Proponent of Radical Theological Democracy and manager of the True Value, stood up and shouted in a demonstrably un-Unitarian tone, "Who are you to bless me? If I want a stinkin' blessing, I'll go out and get it from the Lord Himself!"

"Dignity," shouted Monsignor O'Brien. "Dignity please. We are in the presence of the Lord!"

Litovchenko refused to relent.

The despairing Monsignor broke into a long lament in an attempt to win over his fellow clerics in his time of need.

"What does it mean," he asked, "when it's hard to say 'God bless' today without irony or insult. What does it mean when it's hard to offer prayer for someone without feeling sanctimonious and overbearing, without suffering estranging looks from the godless who have never imagined that others might not be fellow realists. They imagine I persist in churchgoing out of stubbornness, that I wait for a miracle without really believing it will come."

None of the assembled subscribed to Father O'Brien's crisis of faith. Indeed, after four hours of dispute and fruit cobbler, the council's sole joint resolution was to commend Chef Duchaine's culinary prowess.

To avoid the embarrassment of having accomplished nothing, the council also produced a bumper sticker that read *Jesus Is Lord*.

This paltry effort was soundly scorned. Sabbaday was soon rife with an alternative sticker created by the unrepentant Jack Flaherty that said *Jesus Is Lost*.

To put an end to the tiresome and mortifying antics of the unwashed, the Right Reverend Standish granted Monsignor O'Brien the gracious loan of a replacement Jesus. Unfortunately, the loaner Jesus was too big for the bathtub at Saint Linus. Cramped, bent, and resentful of his demotion, this Jesus was never quite the right fit.

Over the next few weeks, the Monsignor also experimented with a two-dimensional Jesus gifted by the Methodists, who did not have the same Catholic fondness for statuary, and a flickering Jesus hologram.

None of the loaners filled the spiritual void.

All this Jesus-swapping (and perhaps an acute case of cobbler withdrawal) raised Brother Earl's Protestant ire. He sowed a rumor that Monsignor O'Brien had secretly hidden the Jesus in his attic somewhere, pointedly asking in his sermon why Monsignor had never showed them the contents of his attic during the ecumenical council.

At next Sunday's homily, Monsignor O'Brien in turn pointed out that he had no attic in the rectory. In any event, he noted, the statue weighed more than 400 pounds, which would obviate hauling it up three flights of stairs. "To do so would have required a miracle indeed," he remarked.

For the next two Sundays, the holy men traded liturgical barbs. Neither got the spiritual upper-hand. In the meantime, Deputy Braver reported no progress in finding the stolen Jesus, let alone in apprehending the culprit.

This uneasy state of affairs became explosive when a fringe Catholic group that called itself the Holy Figure Defenders snatched the Virgin Mary from the other side of Saint Linus's front lawn. In a public statement through spokesman Dean Feller, proprietor of the Watchworks Tavern, the HFD explained that it had no connection to the theft of the Jesus, but due to the crisis in Monsignor O'Brien's leadership, the HFD had assigned itself the burden of protecting Mary from abduction by, paradoxically, abducting her.

Deputy Braver put his foot down and promptly arrested Feller as a threat to public order. The deputy had been willing to overlook a misplaced Jesus, but this second disappearance hit much closer to home. His own dear mother's name was Mary.

"God help those," he thundered, "who sully her fair name or a strand of hair on her head."

Chief Braver cordoned off vast swaths of St. Linus parish and executed numerous search warrants, including one for the Monsignor's nonexistent attic. When the exasperated Monsignor offered up his breadbox as well—"I actually have one of those, Chief. Do you want to search it, too?"—Chief Braver accepted the waiver of rights. He captured the aforementioned breadbox and a tabernacle besides, his apostasy rendering him unable to distinguish one from the other.

Perched on a spare barstool outside the shuttered Watchworks Tavern, shuffleboard mallet in hand as if he might raise it to part the Red Seas, Flaherty mocked Sabbaday's leading citizens.

"Pride goeth before a fall. Am I right?" he said with unrestrained glee. "I've never claimed to be a perfect person, but for all my failings, I'm an honest crook. If the wages of sin are death, I'm the one making a good faith effort to record the income on my 1040 tax return. Maybe now the deputy and priest might reconsider my confession?"

Jack Flaherty continued his sidewalk harangues. The HFD howled about the abuse of its constitutional rights and warned that St. Linus would soon be stripped bare. Meanwhile, Monsignor O'Brien urged calm.

He appealed to the original thief, urging him understand that the church was the statue's keeper. The Monsignor promised to slap a new coat of blue paint on the inside of Jesus' bathtub shell. He vowed to encourage more frequent visits and devotions of the faithful (if any), if only the statue were returned to its rightful place. There would be no questions asked.

These pleas failed to produce fruit. With Holy Week fast approaching and no sign of the Lord's return, Monsignor O'Brien cornered Gay Tarsy. He felt free to speak with the fruit vendor, since Tarsy wasn't a member of the St. Linus congregation. With Tarsy, the most un-Christian thoughts could be spoken aloud with impunity.

"Tarsy," he pleaded, "you're out and about selling fruit 24-7. Didn't you see anything suspicious that night? Didn't you see who made off with my Jesus?"

Gay Tarsy shrugged, winked, and held a finger to the side of his nose, which was on the small side and cute as a button. Perhaps he had seen the culprit, he intimated, but he'd seen nothing wrong with what he'd seen. He'd gone about selling fruit, as he always had. In short, the theft was none of his business.

"Next time, Tarsy, for the love of God, do tell us if you see anything suspicious," the Monsignor pleaded, and—having certain old-fashioned views of the fastest way to a Jew's heart—he generously overpaid for a bright red apple.

"Will there be a next time?" Tarsy asked.

"No, never," Monsignor O'Brien said, with more conviction than he felt. "I've locked the remaining saints down. They'll have to break them off at the knees if they've any hopes of getting away with them."

Monsignor O'Brien tossed the apple he'd bought from Gay Tarsy into the trees at the side of the road. The Monsignor was no fan of fruit unless and until it had passed through Chef Duchaine's capable hands.

A loud shout emanated from the trees where the apple landed. Guiltily, O'Brien charged through the forest toward the sound. He stumbled into a tranquil little clearing. At the center of the clearing stood Chef Duchaine, who was holding the side of his head and complaining to none other than the St. Linus Jesus that the devil himself had tried to stick the fruit of the tree of knowledge directly into his left ear.

Monsignor O'Brien was crushed, by the mendacity of his cook and that of God Himself.

If the Almighty were going to make his presence known at this tranquil little spot where Duchaine wrought culinary miracles from Tarsy's fruit using only a cast iron skillet, it seemed a matter of common courtesy and respect for hierarchy to stop in first at the St. Linus rectory for a cup of tea. As if the loss of that Vatican appointment hadn't brought humility enough. Monsignor O'Brien withdrew from the clearing and trudged back toward St. Linus, Jesus having been found.

The empty bathtub shell on the front lawn mocked him. It seemed to grow as he approached, until it towered over the church itself. The bathtub blue overtook the halo of sky. Jesus remained in the clearing.

When it began to rain, Gay Tarsy took shelter in Jesus' bathtub. He sold his seasonal produce at such cheap prices that he stood no chance of ever getting rich. Even so, Gay Tarsy was not ungenerous.

At the end of the day, he graciously surrendered his place in the tub to let Monsignor O'Brien, the Right Reverend Standish, Brother Earl Everett, and Gertrude Stein Litovchenko stand for a moment in such capable shoes.

*Gene Goldfarb*

# MY MOTHER'S IN THE HOSPITAL

I live with Aunt Rose's family
for now
while mom's in the hospital,
while they operate on her belly,
while she gets better.
Convalescing they call it,
in clean white sheets with medicine
and smart doctors and nurses
who come in to check something
then leave.

My father hasn't visited me.
He has to work.
I lie upstairs and secretly
wipe my nose on the wall
next to my bed,
smell the funny sweetness
of Aunt Rose's pillows,
peer out the window
at the cantaloupe moon
high on the black table
of the night sky.

Then I hear
a crash downstairs
of pots and pans and stuff.
Aunt Rose applauds
with curses in Hungarian
my mother would share if she
weren't in the hospital.

*Gene Goldfarb*

# SAD

*When I'm sad it don't hurt no place. I just know I'm sad.*

*—Benny*

In the basement of the senior center,
Mike passes judgment, says
he thinks Benny wasn't really sad

or contrite, no, there was definitely
a false ring he detected.

He thinks this guy was a fake
a Marlon Brando, trying to play
moody chic with our emotions.

But the poor kid was only four
years old, we tell Mike.

The boy spoke the lines that
were then written down for him
by an old poet.

Mike winced, said
the boy had no right to be
that sad at his age

and we should look for mature,
real poets who can capture
the true grammar of sadness.

Perhaps, but I think Mike
is a twisting, choking vine

and Benny an unopened blossom
in the cool morning shade.

Both sad yes, but a blossom
one day will open.

*Stephanie Renée dos Santos*

# HAIKU HIJIRI

All glanced up from identical soup bowls as Haiku Hijiri entered the broth house. The only sound winding through the air was the silk cord strum of the *shamisen*, played by the old blind *geisha* seated outside the door.

Haiku Hijiri bowed, his hands in a closed lotus before his chest, his eyes soft like well water. The whole of his body was tattooed with the profound and famous *haiku* of Basho, Onitsura, and Buson.

Upon his forehead:

*In the curlew's cry*
*Sign nor signal can foretell*
*How soon it must die*

The owner whisked over, one hand hovering above Haiku Hijiri's bent back, the other inviting him in. Together they moved, two partridges in ground flight.

Stools scraped the floor, making space for the sage to sit—alone. Turtle egg eyes followed his every move.

Haiku Hijiri folded his weathered fingers, each marked with faded black ink of the city of Nara. He lowered his head and waited for his meal.

Soon, steam rose from his bowl and unfurled in fronds. Haiku Hijiri cupped his palms over its rim, eyes closed, praying in quietude.

Slowly, the sound of chatter and the sucking of noodles resumed in the broth house, like the constant creaking in a forest of bamboo.

Haiku Hijiri set down his dish. He peered into its final stirrings. From his pouch, he produced a thin reed brush, a slate inkwell, a corked bottle of *sumi*, and a scroll of rice paper. He gingerly poured the beetle black ink. Then, he tore off a semi-circle of paper. Again, he looked to the remains of his broth.

The banjo-like lute filled the room with longing. All eyes were fixed on Haiku Hijiri. Elegant lines of calligraphy ebbed into the paper, as the priest painted his poem.

Into the bag his inscribed hand reached to produce a round flat stone. He placed the rock upon his poem of payment and excused himself.

Shuffling to the entrance of the broth house, he turned to the owner. Haiku Hijiri bowed his head with gratitude and mirth, and then slipped away onto the road, like a tree into mountain mist.

The aged blind *geisha* plucked her silk strings, while a group of men played a card game of *uta-garuta*.

The owner, wash cloth in hand, went to the table and slid the stone away:

*Enjoy meals alone*
*As the stone welcomes all storms*
*Weathering one's time*

***hijiri***: (Japanese) holy man

*In Japanese religion, hijiri denotes a man of great personal magnetism and spiritual power, as distinct from a leader of an institutionalized religion. Historically, hijiri has been used to refer to sages of various traditions, such as the shaman, Shinto mountain ascetic, Taoist magician, or Buddhist reciter. Most characteristically, hijiri describes the wandering priest who operates outside the orthodox Buddhist tradition to meet the religious needs of the common people.*

*Michael Fessler*

## IN A JAPANESE COIN LAUNDRY

The poster shows a group of *gaijin*:
There's a tall young man with flat hair.
Next to him is his girl
(her face locked into a smile).
A second young man has his arm
draped around a skinny young woman.
She's poking the ice in her glass with a straw
and is oblivious to him.
Then there's this other kid off by himself
doing absolutely nothing but breathing.
In the middle of the poster is The Product
(a beverage of no necessity).
The poster's tacked to the wall of the coin laundry.
It hangs there like a forgotten influence.

My clothes churn in the porthole. Dryers spin.
I think: How do these agencies
make their choices?
Stack *gaijin*. Stack product. Click. Shoot.
Our ads do the same, I guess:
Camera. Kimono. Cars.

International understanding is bunk—
probably. You wonder nonetheless
whether being foreign-viewed is useful.

What for example, could we take away
from these skewed angles and views?
Here's what I say:
These ads depict us as we'd rather not be seen,
stripped of nuance, without protective props,
in front of so-called "goods"
that have nothing to do with The Good.
In other words, let's face it—cheese!—
We see in these depictions what we think
we aren't, or what we couldn't have imagined
ourselves to be.

***gaijin***: (Japanese) foreigner

*Michael Fessler*

# ALONG THE RIVER

The path begins to widen . . . I tug my scarf
and cap; re-adjust my coat. The ground
is bunched, hard; vegetation's browned.
Heads of lettuce loll above the turf.
Elderly now, I've come out for my walk
along the river. The sky is overcast.
I mouth my usual lament: More past
than future to my life. Always a shock.
Ducks quack. A heron stalks. The river's clear,
baring its pebbled load. Wind, too, is candid.
I keep the pace and think of what I did
and didn't do—and still have to. I hear
the rapids rushing out of sight.
Will there be time enough to put things right?

*Diane Vreuls*

# DIRECTIONS

To find the way you have to know the way:

i.
To arrive at the temple gate you stop at an inn;
hear voices, the ring of pots in an inner room,
and wait.

ii.
When no one comes
you join two travelers passing on the road.
They turn up a mossy path, climb through pines
past the sound of water that is not rain,
the tock of wood striking wood
and bells shaking the branches.
Stones, piled on stones, and lanterns line the path.
These may be shrines, or only stones.

iii.
Speaking in their language,
small winds busy the firs.

iv.
The ascent steepens.
We have lost sight of the travelers.

v.
In the clearing we find
no building,
no shrine,
only ourselves emerging.

vi.
Have we lost our way
or found
the temple?

*Nate Fisher*

# SAMSKARAS (IMPRESSIONS)

i.

My tongue flattens against the word,
        and I wonder
        if my head is a pumpkin,
        then what would speaking mean
        to a pumpkin?

A veil, wet with incense and rose oil, coaxes my heavy brow down to my chest. My head bows, so that the throat is closest to the heart.

I cough, mouth a sharp vowel against the damp cloth, the sound of a thousand doorknobs rattling, their locks filled with white persimmon stones and

the book that named me
open, snug on my parent's lap and
breaking into my backbone.

What to call something at first sight?
          There's violet and gold and
          tree. The scarlet ibis, a woman in indigo,
          the rainwater that will befriend.

There are tears on mother's thumbs from
behind a rocky glass of nightgown brandy.
She jabs a fountain pen into her wrist
saying, *Baby, lose something just to look for it.*

ii.
Telephone distance one can hold
in relief, green onion in sugar water
memory, a white cat's desire:
...Sorry, come again?

What remains is the idea of a bird
drowning in the bath, awful motions,

the centurion of sleep peeling apart an artichoke,
moonlight swaying in shadows of a shipwrecked library
beneath waves, reefs of moldering volumes

all autographed in my script. I reach out, open a cover
to these pages ferreted by hands,
the hands' grasp bound by eyelashes

mum terror with each touch,
the pox of fallen fingerprints
a shorn limb billowing maroon below me,
stroking up with

one cupped hand and the flash of tidelight.

*Clifford Paul Fetters*

# DUEL

Amid this
tumble-jumble
mess of humans,
this swirling miasma
of moral fumbles,
a cruelty so adept
it defies mental concept
duels with a love
so stupefying
reason rejects it.

*Clifford Paul Fetters*

## OUTSIDE THE HOUSE

I must tell you, I love the colors.
They make sitting and looking
like being at a live museum,
like just sitting and looking
counts for something worthwhile—
Jerusalem reds, the yellow trumpeters, the pink
bougainvillea, the white gardenia
and its light-headed aroma,
the green, green of all leaves: palm, grape, live oak;
even the little orange pouches of the lizards,
tiny balloons blown in and out.

I live here in circles of color,
knowing full well the grey and the black.
I do not betray the dark truth.
Sooner or later the starless night comes unimpeded.
I've seen shadow cross the crosses,

yet these brights are honest, too. They tell of another truth.

*Dian Duchin Reed*

# CROOKED CUP OF AWE

*Based on the Tao Te Ching, translated from the Chinese*

## LIKE JADE (39)

In the past, all was at ease—
sky because it was clear
earth because it was tranquil
soul because it was nimble
valleys because they were full
living things because they grew
powerful people because they were dedicated.

Wholeness was the result. If things were otherwise,
the results would probably differ—
sky would split off
earth would be a wasteland
soul would call it a day
valleys would be drained
living things would perish
the powerful would be overthrown.

To avoid these catastrophes,
what's precious should use what's common
as a foundation, and the people at the top
should see those at the bottom
as a base.

Yes, the mighty should honor
the lonely, abandoned, and hungry,
but it's now considered wrong to use the humble
as a starting place. Wrong?
Those without eminence merit most.

Jade longs for nothing. A chunk of jade
is as good as a fine jade necklace;
a necklace is as good as a rock.

## NO NEED (51)

The path brings things to life; kindness raises them;
the world shapes them, and outward appearances result:

so of course all things respect the path
and consider kindness precious,

not because they must,
but because it's only natural, for the fact is,

the path conceives them; kindness grows them,
rears them, brings them up, shelters

and stuns them, looks after them
and overwhelms them, and even though

the path engenders, it doesn't possess,
and even though kindness does deeds,

it has no needs; no,
it tends its herds, yet never harvests—

which is why it's called
mysterious kindness.

## USING WHAT'S HERE (54)

The experts at setting things up
will not be left behind. The experts
at cherishing will not fade away.
Those who come after
will thank them forever.

Construct your life of kindness
and be constant. Build a family of kindness
and abide. Cultivate a hometown of kindness
and exist forever. Make a nation of kindness
and be inexhaustible. Create a world
of kindness and be all-embracing.

So use your own life to define what
life suggests. Use your family to mean
family. Use your hometown to signify
birthplace. Use your country
as the concept of nation. Use your world
to represent a living planet.

What do I use
to know the world correctly?
I use what's here.
I use it now.

## HARMONY (55)

To be suckled by kindness nourishes
with more flavor
than milk that newborn babies drink.

Those who drink of kindness
perceive kindness, not
noxious insects with vicious bites,
savage beasts with fearful claws,
plundering birds ominous as storms.

Babies have weak bones and soft muscles,
but a strong grip on things.
They know nothing yet about the parts
that join to make a whole—male-female,
hill-valley, key-keyhole—yet all babies
grow proficiently.

The result of babies' howling
at the end of the day is not hoarse throats,
but harmony and peace. To know
harmony is said to be common
for babies. To know what's common
is said to be enlightened. Being born
brings benefits.

When the mind issues instructions
for breathing, it makes an effort
instead of letting the body do what it does
naturally. Such a mind is strong but stubborn,
which means it's not on the path.
It will spend a long time not on the path,
until it is on the path.

## MORE WORDS (56)

Those who are aware
don't talk about it.
Putting things into words
is not awareness.

Those who are aware
relax their vigor and dispel confusion.
They reconcile light
with the world of dust and dirt.

Yes, the name for this is
"mysterious oneness." That's why
those aware don't need to be
anyone particular. They may be

your intimate,
or else your most distant, relation.
They're doing you good, or else
they're causing no trouble. Perhaps
they're valuable, perhaps insignificant.

In the end, they make
the whole world precious.

*Joe Baumann*

# WHISPER

Mother rises, floats from the couch into the kitchen, leaves you alone on the floor to stare up at the television. When she snaps on the overhead light, small circles of shadow appear beneath her feet.

Water courses from the sink faucet. Mother's shoulders shake, as she scrubs dinner's plates and glasses. The dishwasher is old and broken, a little tomb that sits empty except for the two dish racks and a plastic silverware basket.

Thrust your hands up between the couch pillows, and bend your knees under the afghan draped across your body. Feel a slight tug on the fabric. Glance down and see Whisper curling into a ball behind the crook of your knees.

Look toward the kitchen. Watch Mother hover from the sink to the refrigerator, where she fishes out a can of soda. Say nothing. Watch the cat groom herself, rough tongue poking over the patchy hair of her legs: She's licked them nearly bald, a compulsion she developed in old age.

Whisper's coat was once shiny. The calico fur rippled and gleamed in the sunshine, as she rolled over in the afternoon light to warm her white belly. Now, her underside is bare, the bones and tendons of her lower legs visible against the skin., and half her weight gone.

Remember when Whisper would follow you to the couch, where you hunkered down to watch television after school. She stared up at you from the floor, until you patted the space on the cushion next to you and whistled for her.

Father would stare at you and declare that Whisper was the weirdest animal he'd ever seen, afraid of birds and insects rather than ravenous to capture and eat them.

When she grew too old to hop up onto the overstuffed couch, you started lying on the floor near the television, even though your neck kinked after an hour. Whisper would curl up against your stomach, stare at you, and purr; you would watch her ribs accordion in and out, feeling the bones when you ran your hand down her back, little strands of hair left behind on your palms and fingertips.

One day, she stopped purring. Soon, she no longer sat up by your stomach. She opted to drape herself across your knees, instead. Later, she simply wrapped herself into a ball behind your legs, her head resting on the worn beige carpet. Finally, she no longer came to you, resting instead beneath a table.

Until tonight. She reappears. This night, you'll discover tomorrow when you come home from school, is the last night before she dies.

⌘

Force open the uncooperative front door—the deadbolt sticks—and find Mother floating in the foyer, bobbing up and down as she does when she stays still for too long. Her arms are folded, her eyes bleary and sad.

"What?" you say, kicking off your shoes and dropping your backpack next to the double doors that lead to your father's office. The doors don't latch. Sometimes, Whisper stands up on her hind legs and pushes the doors open, before climbing onto the box in front of the window, where she paws at the blinds until someone pulls them high enough for her to see through.

Mother takes a deep breath and looks away. She stands, rubbing her arms from shoulders to elbows.

"Mother."

She avoids your gaze. Her words come out slowly at first. Then, she rushes into telling you: Whisper couldn't get up to eat this morning, her body an anchor, her head straining forward, the ligaments of her neck taut. Tears form in Mother's eyes when she tries to explain what Whisper's meowing sounded like.

You've never seen Mother like this before, not even when Grandfather passed away. You sat next to her at the funeral, and she was stoic, even able to smile and squeeze your hand when you, ten years old, started to fidget.

"What happened?" you ask, your voice cracking.

She recounts calling the vet, her fingers trembling as she pressed the buttons on the phone. She mimes the action. Her hand shakes like a twisted sheet in heavy breeze.

"Where's Whisper?" you say. Your legs feel heavy.

Mother opens and shuts her mouth, stares down at the floor. See the gray roots in her hair. She mumbles as she tells you she took Whisper to the vet, first scooping her up, wrapping her in a blanket, and laying her in the plastic carrier. Mother tells you the cat's only resistance was a plaintive meow that sounded like air escaping a leaking beach ball.

The doctor had told Mother it would probably be best to put Whisper to sleep.

When Mother says this, you look into the living room. You wait for Whisper to appear, perhaps perched under the high legs of the piano or slumped in a ball beneath the coffee table.

She doesn't slink into view. Feel the weight in your legs intensify.

Reach forward and grip the knob on one of the double doors, forcing your body to remain above ground, your socks slipping against the floor.

Hear your father whistling. Father stops whistling when his head pops into view. For a moment, hate him for making that whistling noise, for the calm and casual warmth he emanates. Imagine his head shrinking, curling up like a little old pea, and disappearing into the ground completely.

Mother and Father stare at you, silent.

Try to catch your breath. Fight the urge to sink into the floor.

⌘

At dinner, watch Father sprout from the floor, his head appearing beneath the green recliner that has been his spot in the living room ever since the room was redecorated. Ratty couches with plaid upholstery, the edges shredded by cat claws, sit still in the basement.

See Father wriggling through the chair. See his head pop up through the slit in the cushioning. See his arms weave through either armrest. One arm hooks to gather food with his fork. He tilts his head to the left until the metal tines meet his mouth. His movements are puppet-like.

At first, the younger sisters don't speak. Then, they start laughing at a sitcom on TV; they gossip with your mother about school.

Your plate balances on the heavy pillow in your lap, as you slump against the couch cushions. Mother slides down between the love seat and the coffee table. Her knees bonk the wooden underside of the tabletop.

Expect Whisper to crawl down the hallway from wherever she's been sleeping, to sit next to Mother and stare, head cocked, meowing every now and then for a bit of food.

Know that she isn't coming. The cage Mother used to take her to the vet sits next to the fireplace, empty, its metal door swinging open ever-so-slightly. The blanket is neatly folded, brushed clean of Whisper's hair.

The family eats early. The setting August sun still shines. It descends through the treetops at seven o'clock when you all walk out the front door in a loping line, a funeral procession of flip-flops, tennis shoes, and khaki shorts.

Mother holds the large shoebox containing Whisper's body, floats across the doorjamb, and lands on the concrete slab that serves as front porch. The space is bare, covered in a dusting of dead insects and crushed leaves. The only decor is a high-backed wicker chair your mother pulled from somebody's garage and a battered welcome mat decorated with muted pink tulips.

Watch as your father follows Mother and emerges through the doorway. He shoots up to full height, like some monolith rising from a receding sea. From his shoulders cascade dust and cobwebs, an avalanche of gloom whisked up into the warm air of late summer. Father and Mother look at one another with warmth, their eyes level. Behind you, the sisters whisper to one another in hushed voices that disappear into the sky.

The hole Father dug before dinner is around the side of the house. The yard slopes downward in a gentle hill. Under a squat, wide tree whose branches reach out and dip so low they form a green dome around the trunk, see a brown grave the size of shoebox.

Stand with your arms crossed. Watch as Mother sets the small box snug into the hole. She lets it fall the last few inches. The box smacks against the earth. The thump of its fall makes you cringe.

No one speaks as Father shovels dirt into the hole. Watch as he pats down a dull, brown hump on the earth.

He leaves the dirt displaced by the shoebox in a messy clump next to the grave. Think of it as a marker, a melted cross that will drizzle down the slope of the yard with the next rains, tears that will dry off in the late summer sun.

⌘

Father watches television with his head perched on the indented back of his recliner. He asks how school is going.

All you can do is mumble monosyllables: Fine. Good.

Look at your father. Indoors, you never see him stand upright. You haven't watched his legs flex and bend to walk down the hallway in years, not since his parents died only a few weeks apart.

Remember the look in his eyes when he arrived home from work the day you had to pack a last minute bag, throwing wrinkled t-shirts and mismatched socks into a suitcase, while Mother corralled the sisters into the car. His eyes were hollow, sunken, and dark.

After returning from your grandfather's funeral, Father disappeared, sinking into the carpet. Mother squeezed your shoulder, nodded, and left the ground. The sisters curled their fingers through their hair and bit their lower lips. Now, Father only appears in full when he goes on his way to work, out to dinner, or to a baseball game.

"Are you okay?" He looks at you and half-smiles.

Get up from your spot on the couch. Feel Father watching you as you cross in front of the television and walk past him. Frustration burns your forehead. Feel your feet sinking into the carpet.

You know that the death of your cat is nothing like Father's loss of his parents. Mother will adopt another cat, or perhaps two. She doesn't like it that Whisper was alone for so long. You feel guilty for being sullen. You feel like your blood is pooling in your feet and sloshing over the nubs of your bones. You can't shake the anger pressing on your shoulders, the anger that started to heat your face at dinner, when all thought of your cat seemed already to have melted from the rest of the family.

In your room, peer out the window. Press the left side of your face up against the glass. See the outstretched branches of the tree under which Whisper is buried, the outline of the leaves blustering in the air, illuminated by a nearby street lamp. Before you can stop yourself, you picture Whisper's grave, the claustrophobic cardboard box she's buried in. You imagine her shuddering and waking up.

You hear her howling, the noise echoing against the unyielding walls of her tomb.

The thought makes you tremble. Your stomach churns. It isn't possible that she's still alive, but you keep hearing that muted noise. You have to reach out and grab either side of the window frame to avoid sinking, or perhaps flying away. You're not sure which, but you know you cannot stay in place on your own.

⌘

Three years later, Father hires a landscaper to redo the yard, while you are off at college. Mother doesn't mention this during any of the weekly phone conversations. When you arrive home for summer break, you find two large oak trees surrounded by dark brown and gray mulch in the front yard. A border of red bricks circles each tree, each trunk dead center like a bulls eye.

Ask when this happened, and Mother shrugs. She's hovering over the stovetop and handling a skillet. She finally tells you that they had it done last October, but by the time you came home for Christmas the ground was covered in snow.

Ask why she never mentioned it.

"I don't know. I guess it slipped my mind. Didn't even think about it."

"What about Whisper?"

"Well, we—"

Turn and retreat to your bedroom before Mother can finish.

The bed is wrapped in your familiar navy blue sheets. Your photographs and trophies still stand lined up on your bureau, as you remember them. Run your fingertips over their plastic surfaces, the metal curves cool and the corners slick. A fine layer of dust has settled. It smears off onto your fingertips. The room smells like a museum. Nothing moves. See the plastic display of a life you're slowly leaving behind.

Walk to the window, and press yourself up against it, as you did the night Whisper died. The glass feels cool against your skin, though the hot sun bleeds across the surface. Shut your eyes. Open them again. Look toward the tree beneath which she is buried. The branches have been sheared back.

Something catches your eye. Your breath cuts short. You turn and leave the room, shutting the door behind you.

You run down the hall and out of doors. Through the grass you run, feet bare. Small stones hiding in the yard pinch your soles. You ignore the pain.

As you run, your feet sink into the ground, as if it were a swamp.

Stop at the tree around the side of the house. You find yourself buried up to your knees in grass and dirt.

A cinderblock retaining wall has been erected around the side of the tree where the yard slopes down. Cement rectangles rise out of the earth in a gray semi-circle. Try to breathe.

Whisper's grave, marked only by that brown hump, has been replaced by concrete blocks and mulch. Feel yourself sink further into the ground. You can almost taste the earthworms and the gritty silt.

Stare at the spot where the grave belongs. Try to imagine where they took Whisper when they uprooted the ground, whether Father told the landscapers to be wary of the spot where your dead cat lay. Did they take care to avoid disturbing her when they tore apart the earth, or was her body caught up in the grinding teeth of an earthmover, her thin coffin shredded and crumpled like a balled-up piece of paper tossed into a trash can? Grit your teeth and shut your eyes.

You imagine Whisper. Feel the warmth of her purring against your stomach, the painful bliss of her outstretched claws kneading at your legs.

Things begin to break apart.

A fissure appears next to you. Suddenly, you're rising up out of the ground, the mud and gravel slaking off of your legs. Beneath your feet, a jagged seam spreads open.

Feel yourself leaving. Look around for something to grab onto, though you know you will float away.

Find yourself lifting off of the grass. Watch as the rift that shot across the yard spreads, fracturing and branching out. The earth moans, falls apart.

You're above your house now. You can see the shingles that need replacing and the gutters full of wizened leaves. The trees in the yard shake. Their trunks shudder, tipping as they are uprooted.

Hear the front door open. Turn to see Mother looking around. Finally, she tilts her head up toward you. You're unsure whether she's smiling or frowning, crying or blinking. You wonder whether she will join you before the earth crumbles away.

The house begins to shift and moan, its foundation ruptured by the splitting ground beneath it. You twist, as you twirl up into the air. Debris and mud hover, and gravity melts away. You try to look toward the tree where Whisper should be, wondering if she will rise, her body dancing up through the warm air, the nubs of her worn bones shining in the sun, paws stretching out in your direction, as everything around you ascends.

*Purvi Shah*

# CRUSHED BONES SOUND SIDEWALK. I RECALL BLACK AND BLACK AND BLACK AND TAKE AN ALEVE IN THE RAIN.

*...And now I eat the Aleve tablet, so I am sitting in front of you and speaking. Otherwise, when it's raining, I cannot speak, because of the sickness. When they beat me, my eye socket was fractured. My nose bone was crushed. And I asked the doctor, "When it's raining, when clouds come, why this pain start?"*

*He said, "This is natural. We can't stop it. You can take the painkiller."*

*Now, when it's raining, when it's cloudy, pain start.*

*—Rajinder Singh Khalsa*

Crushed bones sound sidewalk. I recall black and black
and black and take an Aleve in the rain. Pain ripples this heart.
I cannot fix time's torments or morrows;
I take an Aleve in the rain.

My Buddhas of Bamiyan, too,
pulverized rubbles,
marks of unruly students born of axes. Pause:
Study not fractured world but this self torn by self,
terror that re-takes as my people & I leave in the rain.

In darkness, another dark lurking. 1984:
4,000 swept away, this people's river's blood let.

You say: Do not say riot—
If armed, strike unarmed,
brazened fire a butcher,
say, “Nature too finds unnatural to rake a sieve in the rain.”

Fact: The dead cannot bury nor burn the dead.
Such violence unspilled can neither birth nor quell itself.
Thus: Generation bears horror,
times of youth stolen as even our elders cannot
wake or bereave in the rain.

I say no jail is a justice but just proof of an injustice
now jailed. Joined to this one body,
I bargain selves & time for last plea
just as I both break and forgive in the rain.

Our old poets bespoke monsoon,
charted agony of lovers’ separations,
summoned parting clouds of amassed sorrows.

When I cannot see, when I may not meet your eye,
say then yet in my heart’s tent I offer
and make a reprieve in the rain.

Ask not for peace but its presence in both twined:
neither Rajinder nor Purvi, poet nor saint,
guilty nor innocent, one nor another:
Know now this world of all the above
makes truth such that we must at once
harm, forsake, or alone believe in the rain.

*Ayaz Daryl Nielsen*

## UNTITLED

Of a cloud,
of a dream,
of our journeys—
the emptiness
of all things.

*K. Prasad Kumariya*

# MONKEYS, MIRACLES, AND MEANING

*"Fully-realized sages behold as equal*
*a cow, an elephant, a dog,*
*as well as an outcaste and a Brahmin."*

*vidyavinayasampanne brahmane gavi hastini*
*suni caiva svapake ca panditah samadarsinah*

—*Bhagavad Gita* V:18

From India came another video-record of a miracle. The video-record of the miracle came by way of an old college friend, a fellow science major. The link he sent revealed villagers gathered about a small hut, raising a cloud of chatter as the recorder pressed in for a view.

A macaque emerged from the forest nearby some days ago and hovered over a month-old infant, shooing flies away from the child's face. She grimaced threats at strangers who ventured too close, cuddled the child's crib in her arms, and attended quietly as the child napped.

Amazed villagers observe and test the young female. They exclaim to one another, smile, and laugh. These people are talking about miracles.

With the link came my friend's statement to dispel this miracle: "There is a scientific explanation regarding primate behavior. The young female ape is likely low-ranking, of an age where she desires her own offspring. In such individuals, this sort of adoptive babysitting is common within their own species. Perhaps this female is particularly low-ranking and was rejected as auntie by her cohorts, and so is seeking to fulfill that need elsewhere. This sort of behavior is natural."

So that's that. Once a rational cause is pointed to, most dispense with miracles, disappointedly or jubilantly. Explanation is not negation, though. What is natural is mysterious and wonderful. Maybe, we shouldn't be surprised when another primate acts like we do.

The true miracle can be seen from another point of view. A young female ape wants to have her own child. Perhaps she is rejected by her own kind, has recently lost an infant of her own, or is too young to mate. Wanting to practice mothering in the role of babysitter, she looks out from the forest and sees another species.

The ape sees a woman in a *sari* tending a child and keeping house. The ape recognizes the woman as "like me." The ape sees a baby in the arms of the woman and sees "like my baby."

The ape sees a family. The ape sees its own species from across millions of years of divergent evolution, and recognizes an opportunity. The ape makes a decision to cross boundaries of fear and differences. She decides to cross over to join in common cause.

An ape, without language, without *guru* or religion, without instruction or any of the advantages that bring us toward an enlightened state of peace and unity, recognizes strangers, other animals, what is foreign, as "self." The ape sees another family as "self," sees another's baby as "self," and so becomes part of their world as if this were the natural course of things. And this is the natural course of things.

On the other hand, humans with all the advantages leading to knowledge and understanding are astounded by the idea of another animal as "self." We don't often see another family, another species, or another person as "self." So, we do not cross boundaries with ease as if this were the natural course of things.

Humans live at odds with one another, with other species. When the natural course of things makes itself evident in contrast to human biases, humans cry out in astonishment.

The true miracle is that some monkeys manifest what is holy and beautiful as well or better than humans. Monkeys do so, despite being deprived of everything we think of as superior human qualities; many humans, despite their self-proclaimed superiority, do not manifest so well as monkeys what is holy and beautiful.

When a spiritual friend sent me photos from *darshan* given by a saint in India, I was not surprised to see a langur sitting pensively before the *guru* and listening. I was not surprised to see the langur manifest as Hanuman-ji, receive sweetly the saint's blessing, and then return gently his own blessing on the saint. I was not surprised by the exclamations of "Miracle!" attached to the message.

I can almost hear my other friend again offering an analysis: "These sorts of greeting gestures are natural to langurs and other apes. Music and soft speech do calm animals, wild or domestic. Even while meditating in the forest myself, I have experienced the calm curiosity of animals about this unusual state of serenity. They are naturally attracted to that calm, radiant compassion. Does this make for more of a miracle or less of a miracle?"

My spiritual friend went on to say that she was at Haridwar, staying in a home protected by iron-barred windows, when a langur reached through the bars and tried to claw her arm. The householder called to her, pulling her away from the langur just in time to save her from a nasty scratch, and maybe a bite and infection as well.

Like those of Haridwar, the monkeys at Hrishikesh are accustomed to the flux of pilgrims. As do pickpockets and beggars, they gather to see what they can get from tourists. They get what they can by every method that people do: by sneaking and snatching, by threats and tricks.

Why do these monkeys leave the forest and behave like what we call *criminals*? Their forests have been taken by humans. Like criminals, the monkeys are pressed by hunger and the sight of bounty. They live meagerly, and they are tempted by excess.

The monkeys living in shrinking forests, where people tear down the trees to build their own homes. The monkeys see houses full of food and warmth. They see these houses as shelter from tigers, snakes, and hawks.

In Haridwar, my friend did not cut down the forest, nor did the langur build her host's house. My friend and the monkey inherited this *karma*. They are both only partly aware of their contributions to this conflict. They are both pressed by wants and needs. Neither can reverse the situation; both can opt to do differently from now on.

We do not recognize these other primates as "self." So, we leave the monkeys to suffer and find relief in extinction. We do not even recognize other humans—the criminals, the desperate, the poor, the oppressed, and neglected—as "self."

We ignore them or deprive them of their freedom and even their lives, leaving extinction as their relief.

So, my friends, one primate ends up behind a barred window that holds plenty and comfort, while another primate is closed out in a world of desperation and extinction. On neither side of the bars is the true self, the *atman*, recognized.

That's no miracle.

A miracle is when this does not happen.

*Barbara Wuest*

## NO TOMORROW

Early December and just before dark, You
move in on me, move in on my thoughts
about childhood and children at play—

It is early in Baghdad, the young ones
asleep, covers pulled up to their chins,
lost in their dreams of ancestors and God

—yet to live the now of the trusting child
requires that I give up endings and plots
and worries disguised as forms of control.

It's to live as if there are all the tomorrows
my brain and heart and soul can possibly
conjure and no tomorrow anywhere at all.

My window darkens to the scene outside.
Snow-laden birches have lost their light.
The moon is blocked, the lamplight dead.

I can see into my sin and decay.
I do not tremble in the face of ruin
and wrongdoing on a bright day.

Still, the grace of the sun on a snowy branch,
the safe awakening of the world's kids,
food delivered for the Sudanese poor—

these are three of the dreams that slide through
my battle within, the country's without,
bearing scant peace until we each can meet.

It's tomorrow for the young ones asleep
in their family homes, gone from their
cities for a time, and dreaming of God.

I never do anymore, afraid I will drop
my guard and drown in the knowledge that
the You I address is the same as their God,

that their buried relatives are just as much
mine, that their primitive faith is the one
I seek, that the voice I am after is as plain.

*Abigail Carl-Klassen*

# REINCARNATION

Twenty-four hours after leaving Kolkata, my husband and I arrived in Varanasi with our friends Josh and Susan. We were refreshed by our Tier Three Air-Conditioned Class train ride. We had treated ourselves after three weeks of volunteering at a hospice in Kolkata.

What a difference $15.00 extra apiece bought us. Sheets. Pillows. Blankets. There was none of the fighting or screaming we'd experienced in Second Class, where fifty people were shoved into a compartment. The lights were even turned off at night, so that we could sleep.

That evening, we decided to go out on the Ganges as the sun set. We would watch the cremation fires light up the shore. They would cast shadows upon the ancient stone alleyways of Varanasi, one of the oldest continually inhabited cities in the world.

While we walked along the shore on the way to the boat, strangers waved and shouted at us, "The holiest city in India. A very good place to die!"

Varanasi is a city of temples, religious scholars, and *sadhus*. In Hindu cosmology, this city is considered to be the center of the earth; it is the place where two holy rivers, the Ganges and the Assi, converge.

Hundreds of thousands of Hindu pilgrims travel to Varanasi each year to bathe in the river that rids them of sin.

Funeral pyres burn on the shore twenty-four hours a day. Hindus believe that once a person's ashes are returned to the Ganges, his or her soul is free from the cycle of death and rebirth. After cremations, family members bathe downriver to receive the good *karma* from the released relative.

On the shore, children play cricket. Cows wander in and out of the river, and vendors approach tourists with their wares.

Josh and Susan bought two butter wax candles surrounded by flowers in banana leaf baskets. They bought these from a bald, swollen-bellied street child who ran up behind them yelling the phrase interchangeable for any occasion in India, "Hello! Hello!" They also bought a picture postcard book of the city.

The child continued to shout, "Hello! Hello!" until they took his picture and showed him his face illuminated on the back of their camera.

Josh and Susan waited until we had drifted in the boat to the middle of the river before lighting their two candle baskets. One was for a man they'd cared for at the home for the dying in Kolkata. Another was for those burned in the mass electric crematoriums of Varanasi. Those who could afford it were burned in wood fires.

Once, while on shift at the hospice, Josh was asked to help move a man who had died during the night from the hospice's cold storage to the crematorium. The crematorium was so far away that they would need to ride in one of the organization's blue-and-white ambulances to get there.

After Josh had helped prepare the body for cremation, he turned to walk into the street. He planned to wait while the body burned.

The man who flipped the switch to turn on the fire beckoned and said said, "No, brother. Come. Watch."

As the electric fire burned, Josh didn't know which he felt more uncomfortable about—the fact that he was watching the cremation of a stranger or that he, a Westerner, felt unsettled watching fire consume flesh.

His experience caused me to question my own discomfort about death. I began to wonder if perhaps cremation was not a destruction of the body, but an illumination of life, like the lighted baskets released into the Ganges.

I watched Josh and Susan's candle float away in the darkness. Suddenly, I had an inexplicable desire to release a basket of fire into the Ganges. It was as though all the spiritual energy surrounding the city had sparked an exhilarating divine connection within me. I hadn't felt like this since leaving my job as an Evangelical lay minister.

Since we had already set off into the water I didn't say anything.

It wasn't long before long our boat was surrounded by vendors. Teenage boys and young men walked from boat to boat. They balanced their bare feet on the prows and the merchandise on their heads or fingertips. "Chai? Chips? Picture books? Candles? Best price!"

My husband asked me if we wanted to buy a candle basket. He seemed to know instinctively what I was feeling.

Before I could answer, he called one of the vendors over. The teenager wore a white undershirt rolled up to his chest because of the heat.

My husband insisted that we needed only one basket and that we didn't need any picture books. Then, he placed the basket in my hands and said, "Maybe we can light it for our grandmothers."

He hadn't known his mother's mother, because she'd died young from complications of rheumatoid arthritis. When she died, his mother finished raising the rest of her siblings. She'd begun raising them years earlier, because her mother was unable to lift a pot or scrub a floor. His grandmother was buried with her rings on, though she could never wear them while she was alive.

My grandmother had died last February, after spending her last days in a nursing care facility for the mentally ill. Diagnosed with schizophrenia when she was forty, she had pulled a knife on a woman at a laundromat. The woman said she wouldn't press charges, if my grandmother got help.

My grandmother started smoking after having her last baby. She lit chain after chain of cigarettes while institutionalized, until her social worker said she wasn't allowed to smoke with her oxygen tank.

My grandmother's doctors said that the congestive heart failure was brought on by thirty years of anti-psychotic medications. They kept her away from cigarettes, from fire—from destruction and from illumination.

I watched the river's procession of light. I felt that releasing a burning basket into the river with all the others could help my grieving. The grief had begun when my grandmother had died, on Valentine's Day. It had never been brought to any sense of completion.

I'd tried to figure out a way to bring her with me everywhere, not just to my wedding which took place nearly a year after her death. I'd wanted to bring her to India and to every place that she couldn't go when she was alive and chronically ill. I'd wanted to bring her to my high school and college graduations.

I wanted to take her away from the drunken husband who had locked her in the basement and beat her. He beat her because she burned his dinner, because she said "hello" to another man, because the kids caught goldfish and swam them in the bathtub.

I wanted to take away the voices and the visions and Tom Brokaw's secret messages hidden in the television.

Maybe, I could release these memories into the Ganges where they could rest. Most of all I wanted to honor her.

I wanted to honor her and give her something for all that she had given me. I wanted to honor her especially for what she had given to my mother.

When my mother gave the eulogy at my grandmother's funeral, she said that my grandmother was both her father and her mother. With my grandmother's death, my mother was orphaned. My grandmother's death was two deaths instead of one.

Burial in the Ganges is for those most revered. Perhaps, such a burial is for a person who was more like two people than one.

Although my grandmother was buried in the February snow of rural Illinois, I carried her with me now. Though I had no ashes, I brought her here. I wanted to lay her down here—

with kings and princes and holy men, because that's what she deserved.

My husband struggled to light the candle with a cheap lighter that he'd bought for the cheap Indian cigarettes sold individually at nearly every shop. When the candle was lit, I held it for a moment, and then gently released it. I watched it float away with the other flickering baskets. The sun had set. The night was dark, except for the river of light.

I had not read the *Bible* in more than a year.

*Blessed are those who mourn.*

Now, I repeated these words in my mind like a *mantra*.

I wondered about my grandmother's soul. I wondered if all of the violence and tragedy of her life had truly been released into the Ganges.

I wondered if the cycle of wounding and bitterness would ever be put to rest in me. Did I believe that my life and my faith could be reincarnated? Was it possible for my faith in life to be born again and again and again into something new?

I watched the flames of the funeral pyres on the surface of the river of light. Light reflected upon light. I smoked a cheap Indian cigarette and wondered if there were a place in the Kingdom of God where my smoldering ember could be a lamp on a stand, a light of love that could not be hidden.

*Doug Bolling*

# STILLNESS

At night in the mountains
silence holds the world in its
palm.

The angels that lurk,
the lions and chimeras,
all of them settle about
in the great cloth of
darkness.

We came as sojourners.
We aspired to become what
we had missed in the valleys
and towns far below.

You say: Love is a leaving
behind. It calls us toward
uncertain distance,
horizons yet untouched.

We build a fire on the
narrow ledge, two steps away
from the drop-off.

Our words leave us there
in the high chill of wind
and snow.

We become unknowns, forgetting
our names, how we got
here,

the moments enfolding us
like the great mother
letting us be,
letting us
listen.

**Angel**
Kathleen Gunton

*Matt Schumacher*

# WATTS TOWERS: LOS ANGELES, CALIFORNIA

*For Captain Rodia*

We're
the crew
of the three-
masted ship
christened Watts
Towers, a boatload
of sailors left stranded
in the ghetto instead of adrift
in the ocean. We sailed with Captain Rodia
until his past as drifter and minister disappeared.
Only scaffold and ladder mattered. With his window
washer's
hook,
Captain
Rodia climbed
the air's invisible riggings.
He built two ninety-foot towers
relying solely on their spires for
support, binding them by hand with copper
wire. He sailed his ship on waves melted and woven:
tapestries of broken tile, cracked dishes bought for a penny
from neighborhood children, shattered glass
bottles that once held 7UP and Milk of Magnesia,

scrap metal that had ballasted
freight cars now discarded near railroad tracks.
Our captain constructed
voyages,
firm triangular
forms, curves that
held their place in space
and time. He found solace
in their resilience. His ship
survived earthquakes, El Nino,
and the Watts Riots, though his small house
burned down, ignited by a firecracker. Afterward,
the captain willed his vessel to the lone neighbor who'd
failed to call him crazy. Some say he died ten years later
in Martinez. We know he's out there. Captain Rodia, we're
still sailing these streets. Please lead us to the sea. Come back
from that lotus land. The headless angel points skyward,
seven rungs above
your self-portrait.

*Matt Schumacher*

# EMERY BLAGDON'S HEALING MACHINE: GARFIELD TABLE, NEBRASKA

Emery unlocked the shed's door, and we stepped inside.
There was not a great deal of light.
Masses of wire hung from the walls
and ceiling. The mineral salt bottles sat
around on the table and held little tin flowers.
He opened a padlocked inner door
to the main room, reached
around the corner, threw switches.
Christmas tree lights came on. Some stayed on.
Some blinked on and off, reflecting
off hundreds and thousands of pieces of copper wire,
tin foil, painted tin can lids. The lights
were woven through these constructions. It hit me
all at once: This small room, a vast panorama.

Outside—miles and miles of nothing
but sandhills, a few cornfields, a few cattle.
Here, within this shed, a world.

*Patricia Farewell*

# WORK

He lives alone among wind turbines and fields of rotting
crops. Fixing thickens him, ensures substance.

Nailing an errant tile back onto the roof, assembling
a latch for a door that takes a shoulder to shut it,

then sprawling on the ground to reach the underside
of a fence, he scrapes and paints each summer.

Small hollows where rainwater settles for days
need caulking; big maples want trimming.

Fissures, rust, leaks, and noisy loosenings
find him out and conspire to unnerve him.

Nicked and blistered by sunset, haunches heavy
with sweat and exhaustion, he's on the stoop

wrestling with a work boot that won't come off.
*Dammit*, he shouts. *Dammit*, as if he would be heard.

*Patricia Farewell*

## THIS STRETCH OF ROAD

*Lily and Lady*, *Lily and Lady*,
she loves to say, driving by the sister
mares who'll  foal come May. She loves to flick
the tip of her tongue to the roof of her mouth
and form the L-sounds.

Shoulder to shoulder, the horses stand.
They toss  their manes and swish their tails
to shoo flies.

Insects grazing grasses, children
laughing, cars cupping music—
these sounds surround their pasture.

They've never heard the names she's given them,
riding this stretch of road slow and alone,
saying *Lily and Lady* over and over,
as if these names might cleanse her,
as if she had something to forget.

*Sarah Spivack*

# WITH THE DESERT BY MY SIDE

I sat on the steps at the edge of the veranda and wondered what had changed since I was a child.

The yard was bare, except for a few lone weeds poking up from the dry, dusty ground. The earth sighed with an arid wind that mirrored my melancholy mood. I could almost see myself as a child, playing with dolls among the tumbleweeds.

I had always seen the desert as something to marvel at. Under my imaginative child's eye, the parched ground melded into rich pastures, their endless expanse wide with possibility.

During my early years, I wanted to be an astronaut, an actor, a poet, and the president, all at once. I could, because I still had my whole life ahead of me. My slate was clean, unmarred by love or tragedy, hate or prejudice. All I knew was the desert and the big world beyond our little ranch.

I was still wearing my graduation cap, when I left our ranch to explore the world.

As time passed, this life which had once seemed broad and full of possibility became hollow and meaningless. I began to long for the desert.

I longed for a cold glass of lemonade at sunset. I longed to see the sky, twinkling with a million pinpoints of light. I longed to hear the sound of my mother's voice, telling me to go play; she could do the dishes on her own. I longed for anything familiar, anything commonplace to anchor me, to remind me of who I once was.

I returned to the desert and looked out to the horizon.

All I could see was failure: I saw my father's face, when he heard I'd dropped out of college. I saw my brother's face, when I showed up at his door and asked for money. Most clearly, I saw my own face, pallid, tired, and defeated, as I looked into the bathroom mirror.

Although many years had passed, my childhood remained unchanged. This thought was comforting. I imagined that every desert crack and each single sprout remained untouched. I could step into the past, a dream world where there had been no disappointment, no error. This was a fantasy place with only me, my dolls, and the tumbleweeds.

How I wished I could travel backwards to that time in my life. How I hungered to change so many decisions I had made. My heart sighed. The desert joined in with my regretful cry, merging our two voices into one.

The desert. It had always been my home and always would be. The desert would never let me down. It would remain, singing its mournful song, even as my body crumbled to bits under the scorching sun.

Others in my life would come and go. The desert would stay by my side.

Many storms pass through its plains, and the desert endures. The sun bakes its surface, and the desert endures. Animals dig deep into its skin, and the desert endures.

As my soul will endure.

I close my eyes, let my hair whip about my face.

*Noel Conneely*

## BLUE SOCKS

The beautiful rain falls lightly
into the cottage. Only the roof slates
hold on; the mouse in the attic
has no immediate plans for the future.

The blue socks of the sweet-tongued woman
have holes. If God's ear is big enough
for her prayer, the world may well be saved
from Swiss rolls and Irish whiskey tooraloo.

The woman holds the corner of a fig roll
between her fingers. The body of Jim Figgerty
has been found in a shallow grave in a wooded area
near a well known scenic location. Paramilitary

involvement has not been ruled out.
The DPP is compiling a book of evidence,
and Paddy Power lays odds
the killer won't be found by Christmas,

especially if it's a white one.
None of the smart backers take it up.
The woman with the fig roll licks her fingers,
continues to love dispassionately.

And the lovely rain is falling.
Only the sky knows when it will stop.

*Ryan Rickrode*

# THE HEAVY VEIL OF WIND-DRIVEN RAIN

**On the news they** say there were tornados as far north as Buffalo and Toronto. What I know is, here in Chambersburg, the storm ripped the steeple off the church. We were huddled in the basement in the dark, children crying and deacons praying. To me, it all just sounded like wind.

The state troopers found Karla's body underneath Ralph Farley's pickup in the field across the road. They told us her death would've been almost instantaneous, which is some consolation I guess, except I know she must've still been alive while she was in the air.

John says I should let it go, drop it, leave it be, but he wasn't there. Karla, she was only 24, and not any older than our younger boy Samuel. Last night in bed John, said to me, "Jill, you never even knew the girl. You're just feeling bad because she didn't leave behind a family that you can cook a casserole for." He said, "It's not your fault. What's done is done is done. Get some sleep."

I closed my book and turned out the light. The truth is, I had been thinking of making a dish for the Metzgers, because they'd loved Karla like a daughter. There was no point in explaining that to John.

I rolled over and put my back to him. Sometimes, I wish he would hold me like he used to when the boys were young.

**There hadn't been** a storm like this in Franklin County since May of 1985, when a tornado crossed Route 11 and traveled along Orchard Drive, all the way up to Wayne Avenue, where it tore the roof off the K-Mart. That tornado brought down trees and power lines, knocked a house off its foundation, and shattered all the windows in the Wendy's by the stoplight, but nobody got hurt.

I remember watching the sky turn from marbled grey to ghost-green, while I waited for John to get home from work. Trashcans blew down our street like tumbleweeds.

John got the car under the carport just as the hail started coming down. It was like God had waited until he was safe to really start the storm.

I put on some coffee, and we waited it out in the basement. We curled up together on the old loveseat. I was pregnant with David at the time. I thought John and I would be long dead before another storm like this hit the valley.

**For the funeral, Pastor Matt** came back up from the church he'd started in Virginia and delivered the eulogy. He told us that the early Christian martyrs believed when they suffered, Christ suffered with them. So it was with us.

"We can do all things through him who gives us strength," he said.

I thought his words fell flat. I wanted something more, some assurance that the clouds would clear, that the sorrow would burn off like the dew. He should've spoken about deliverance.

Instead, he told us that God appeared to Job in the form of a whirlwind. A whirlwind. He crossed a line there.

Anyhow, with Karla's body tucked away in the earth and her soul at home with the Lord, I hoped we could all begin limping toward closure.

**If you wanted to be** pessimistic, you could say that Karla's whole life had been one long string of tragedies. Her father was a lazy and abusive drunk. He was out of the picture, thank God, before Karla started elementary school. Her mother worked the day shift at Tip Top Dry Cleaning and the night shift at Denny's. The old townhouse they lived in was only a block away from the church, but her mother never attended our services. She did, however, drop Karla off at the church Wednesday nights on her way to Denny's. The charity she wouldn't accept from us we lavished on her daughter.

Pastor Matt—he was our youth pastor then—took Karla under his wing and added her to his running, shouting, screaming flock. She was a fair-haired wisp of a girl, with pale blue eyes and a ten-gallon smile that barely fit her face.

She was too shy to talk to boys, or most anybody else for that matter. She did take to Walt and Connie's girl, Meg Metzger. Pretty soon the two of them were inseparable. There wasn't a moment when they weren't whispering and giggling to each other.

For a lot of us, the first time we actually heard Karla's voice was when she read the scripture at Meg's funeral: "The Lord has given, and the Lord has taken away. May the name of the Lord be praised."

Meg was killed in a car accident coming back on Route 11 from the drive-in up in Newville with one of the Sanford twins. She was killed by a drunk driver. Both he and the Sanford boy walked away from the wreck.

For a long time after that I wouldn't let Samuel or even John stay out past ten-thirty.

**The Metzgers loved Karla** like she was their own child. They made up their minds to send Karla to college with the money they'd saved for Meg's education. In the fall, Karla started commuting to Shippensburg University. She was studying to be an elementary school teacher.

A year later, her mother came down with lung cancer, of all things. Karla dropped out of school to work full-time, so her mother could quit Tip Top and focus on her treatment.

For our part, we took up a collection each month especially for the two of them. Of course, we prayed for strength, peace, presence, and healing. Pastor Lehman visited Karla's mother every Thursday. The men of the congregation saw to it that her grass got mowed. The rest of us made sure that Karla and her mother stayed well fed.

There's not much that can be done for lung cancer. When the Lord called her mother home, Karla took it hard.

We saw her less and less at Sunday service, and then not at all. She might even have gotten into drugs, but I can't say for sure. What I know is that she fell in with the wrong crowd. The next time we saw her, she was pregnant, just starting to show, with no man in sight. Some fireman from Waynesboro, I heard.

The Metzgers offered to raise the child for her, but she politely declined. She looked pale and thin and older than her years, but she'd made up her mind to raise the child herself.

The baby was a gift is what she told us. I think the pregnancy brought her back to God.

The child was supposed to be a girl. Karla planned to name her Meghan, after Meg Metzger.

Seven months into the pregnancy the child died from complications and was stillborn. Pastor Lehman made the announcement about it just before the morning prayer. I felt sure in my heart that Karla would disappear again. I very much wanted her to disappear, to leave the church and never look back.

There was a candlelight vigil for the child and then a funeral. We all made casseroles, cakes, and jellos, but nobody knew what to say. It wasn't right what the Lord had done. At least, it seemed so to me. I don't know what I'm saying here.

The thing is, Karla didn't disappear again. On the contrary, she didn't miss a single Sunday service. She was always there, fifth pew from the front on the left, immovable as an anchor. It was like she'd made up her mind not to be broken again. Or maybe she had been broken so completely that she could not be broken anymore. Her pieces were too small.

**It was about this** time that I took up the position of Assistant to the Church Secretary. It's minimum wage, a high schooler's job, but I like it. I fold bulletins, type up the directory, and water Pastor Lehman's plants. It gets me out of the house in the evenings, when John comes home and sets up his laptop on the kitchen table. His briefcase is like a bucket that brings home the office, and that laptop screen is like a wall.

Sometimes, I imagine I smell a young woman's perfume running like fingers through his hair. I want to ask him why he isn't finishing his work at the office.

Instead, I go into the church at night, when it's quiet and still. I listen to Delilah on the radio, while I slip inserts into the bulletins. There's rarely anybody there that late at night—I have my own key now—and for a while I felt like the space was my own.

Then, I began to notice Karla's car out in the lot every night, parked near but never next to my old minivan. She would quietly let herself into the church and pray alone in the nursery. Sometimes, she would weep while she was kneeling before the cribs. Now and then, I would look in on her.

With her pale skin lit up red from the glow of the exit sign, she looked almost like a painting of Jesus praying in the garden.

The thought of her looking back at me was more than I could bear, so I never interrupted her, never prayed with her, never rested my hand on her shoulder or stroked her hair or held her the way I would have if she'd been one of my boys. She obviously wanted to be left alone is what I told myself.

God must have been carrying her, though. It was almost miraculous the way she bounced back. Three months after she buried her daughter, she started teaching Sunday School and volunteering with the youth group. She signed up to help in the nursery—that surprised a lot of us. Pretty soon she was volunteering at Pregnancy Ministries and talking about going back to school to finish her degree.

All the while, she was still working full-time at the mall. She'd become like a person turned inside out, radiantly selfless, like a fire or a light bulb. She's so bright you can't look directly at her, I used to say. Look at her too long, and you'll hurt your eyes.

**The clouds in the sky** that afternoon were liquid grey. The haze of a downpour in the distance had us scrambling to get our covered dishes and crock pots out of the pavilion and into the church gymnasium.

Forecasters said the storm would pass north of us, but that didn't stop the rain from coming down in sideways sheets. We were later told that the rain was why we didn't see the tornado form in the field down the road. When it's raining, sometimes you can only see tornados with radar.

The men pressed their puppy-dog faces against the window glass in the lobby. Bats and gloves were piled beside them. They were pointing at something over the cornfield, some strange swirling flock of birds. Afterwards, we learned they weren't birds at all, but shingles and cornstalks.

Karla pulled into the parking lot. The headlights on her car were fuzzy from the wind and the rain. She parked in the closest stall she could find, a good fifty or sixty yards out. She must not have realized there was a tornado. None of us did.

When she popped out of the car, we could barely see her through the rain. There's disagreement among those of us who saw as to whether or not Karla could have escaped had she turned and run when she stepped out of the car—because she must have seen the tornado then, or heard it at least. It sounded like a freight train.

Two or three of the younger men say she could've made it, but I don't think so. Most of us who saw say Karla didn't have a chance.

She looked back at us, gauging the distance. Then, she turned toward the whirlwind. She stood there for a moment with the wind whipping through her hair. She stepped forward to meet the storm, as if her whole life had been only a long preparation for this one moment. I didn't see her get lifted up, knocked down, or struck by Ralph Farley's truck.

I just saw Karla step forward, and then the rain got too thick. That's all. She disappeared.

Someone—not John—grabbed my arm, took me down to the basement, and probably saved my life.

The storm shattered the windows in the lobby with metal it wrenched off of the playground equipment.

**Karla's in the ground** now, buried in the plot between her mother and the daughter she'd wanted so badly. In the weeks and months ahead, we'll limp our way toward closure. I'm confident of that. It may take people like the Metzgers, myself, and Ralph Farley a bit longer than the others, but sooner or later things will settle back to normal. The clouds will clear. The sun will rise. All will be well, by and by.

When John is asleep, I close my eyes to pray, "God, save my marriage," but all I see is Karla. Karla stepping into the whirlwind and quietly vanishing, as if she were only slipping behind a curtain. The image burns sharp and clear, like a candle in a cave. It keeps me awake at night.

*Fran Isaacs Gilmore*

# THE LOON

So heavy it must
run along the water, wings flapping
for nearly a quarter mile
before it can lift.

We have only to unfasten
the heavy chain of self.

*Fran Isaacs Gilmore*

# LAKE, KAYAK, SKY

The bow swings side to side,
carving a zig zag path

as it advances, soundless
but for the dip of the paddle

and its hollow knock on the rim.
An island full of gold,

russet trees, and noisy crows
approaches, recedes.

I plunge my mind into the water,
let the shock of cold

silence it. Words fly off like
birds and disappear.

*Charlotte F. Otten*

## KAYAKING ON HALF-MOON BAY

He had gone to Prince William Sound
for a two-week course on sea paddling,
but the sea turned sullen,
pelting rain at this novice kayaker,
hitting him from above
not below.

Crestfallen,
he had to get away from Alaska
to try kayaking again.
California called.
Half-Moon Bay beckoned.
Known as a Paradise of Breakers,
it taunted him to take a risk.

Heaving and reeling,
waves the height of skyscrapers
shoved him off course,
challenged him to see the world
from the heights—

conspired, sprayed the horizon with mist,
forced him into torrent tunnels.

*sun glints on the waves*
*darkness on the face of the deep*
*sea lions oblivious of his plight*
*dance on the swing of the sea*

Hands squeezing the paddle,
he jabbed, stabbed, slapped watery air
as he plunged with the bow of the kayak

*he flips, rises, grabs his bearings*
*swings out of the waves*
*glides on slack water*

and landed on a safe patch of shore.
He kissed the sweet earth
with the glee of a quavering Jonah.

*Susan Azar Porterfield*

# POINT WITH CONNECTING LINES

*...and sudden returns when we thought*
*we would never see each other again.*

*—Jose Saramago*

A rock on the island of Iona
may or may not exist.
It was hot, odd
for Iona,
and I sat on the strand
on a low, level stone
along the dock
to escape my shoes for the waves
dancing.
A small, brown dog was happy there.

*Paul B. Roth*

## FEELING IT

This silence
and a red-bellied woodpecker's tapping
echo the way stomachs swell
with the rattle of hunger

Swooping across country roads
lone crows
from ripening cornfields
strut all-night pharmacy parking lots

Gazing at your hands
you wonder if they'll ever lose the urge
to jerk-start chainsaws
to squeeze the herbicide gun's
easy trigger
in favor of feeding the weakest voices

Though brief
you wonder if earthworms
glistening in the sun
will ever escape becoming tragedies
whose motions unwrite themselves

You wonder if ripples
if winds trace this silent shore
if they will blend with the secrets
sacred tree rings keep
or simply wrinkle the reflection
your absent face
has suddenly become

*Paul B. Roth*

# ALLOWANCES

If you let me
I'll be this light set before you

If you let me
I'll be what comforts you when at times
the current universe
exploding inside the rough wall of a sand grain
is ground between the rusty pliers' teeth

If you let me
I'll be the night set before you
sweeping a path of stars
around the moist sides stones hidden
from the dry ring of your footsteps

If you let me
I'll be the mourning dove's
outstretched wings
fanning sunlight through the illumination
of your true name

If you let me
I'll be the black-capped chickadee's
scratchy feet poking your palm
and fluttering its wing feathers
against the last things
your fingertips remember touching

If you let me
I'll be hibiscus flower purple
held up to the mirror at the beginning of your skin
where the pulse and zip of hummingbirds
loop
through your unrestrained bloodstream

If you let me…

*Katherine West*

# ORNITHOLOGY

*In the shadow of your wings, I am ecstatic.*

*—Psalm 63:5.9*

i.

***ranan***: (Hebrew) "...strong feelings of emotion, exultation and ecstasy, which may then break out into verbal expression...a meditative technique where one binds to the divine with all of one's emotions."

—Areyh Kaplan

Elegant white calls red secrets sky to sky while we bang on the glass box rattle panes in sockets eyes rolling like horse's mad with flame rearing hooves punching holes in morning's vein of sap rising like honey in the throat in the blue ear of spring are you listening to the wind blowing in teeth in ears under fingernails around the neck like a scarf of ice late winter long underwear in the drawer at home windows cracked critical mass wafting over the sill seeping into the flesh of walls into the flesh of flesh a flushed and ruffled look alert turn of head flash of eye we leave the windows open.

ii.

***shasha***: (Hebrew) "…rapt attention, where one is oblivious to all outside influence…something that is rapidly repeated… to chirp…to flutter…a constant oscillation of concentration, a continuous turning on and off of one's attention."

—Aryeh Kaplan

Restless bluebirds landing retreating approaching muttering like a fickle breeze forward and back forward and back against scraped sky *tsunami* peaks booted feet rest makes a circle stasis makes sun close makes blue keep moving makes you so transparent I can see your thin bones your *shtetl* ears beneath your wool cap your *kabbalah* eyes closed in meditation as the sun leaches you from yourself while above one kestrel beats and beats white from below with black on the tail fanning out to rise closing up to descend sun behind like a candle with wings face to face we hover above our shadows on snow so when the dive finally comes a blow to the chest grunt gasp and the kill is made just as you awaken.

*M. J. Roberts*

# HAWK

*Behind all this, some great happiness is hiding.*

—*Yehuda Amicai*

I see him atop a telephone pole, his silhouette familiar by now. I don't know why, but I assume he is male, that he is the same red tail hawk I've seen in the past.

I see him often, when I walk on this path in the Santa Monica Mountains, alone, in silence, attentive to the earth, sage, and rocks. He is sometimes circling above me, sometimes resting on the power pole, his head rotating, one eye holding me in his gaze.

I stop and bow my head his direction. If I speak, he hears me out before he spreads his wings and lofts himself into the air with ease and grace. I can almost feel the moment when the sky catches him.

"It may be enough to see just one thing," my teacher has said.

Is this what she means? I do see him in a way I see very few things in this world. What is most mysterious about these meetings with the hawk, however, is not just that I am seeing but that I feel seen.

Sometimes, when I journey to the *shaman's* drums, I nestle into the feathers of my guide and fly with him. He shows me what it feels like to be other, to see through different eyes.

Those are waking dreams, teachings. This is a flesh and blood hawk that hunts, sleeps, and mates in the mountains above Malibu. He has a heart and belly, feathers that molt. His talons kill; his beak tears flesh. His eyes search for the scurrying beasts that fear him and the gross beings like me that he must fear.

In the moments when my eye connects with the hawk's, I feel an opening, a threshold between worlds which either of us could cross. Possibility quivers between us—me stepping into him, him flying into me.

The moment passes. He spreads his wings and lofts himself into the air. I watch him become a speck and disappear beyond the hillside. I walk on.

The next morning while I'm meditating, not thinking about that hawk or my breathing or anything, from out of nothing it seems the hawk appears, the hawk of my mountains—the cross of his body and wings spreading out before me as he flies right through my ribcage, so that his own heart beats against mine. I feel the weight of him, and I realize: I am not afraid.

We stay like this for the space of one breath, then another, then another. Even though the hawk's presence is outside of my ordinary experience, it doesn't feel uncomfortable.

I've wanted to know what it's like to see the world through the eyes of a hawk; maybe the hawk wanted to know how it feels to live inside a being like me, to feel with a human heart.

I expect him to leave when I finish the meditation, but he wants to stay with me. Okay. I move through the day, acting as I normally act: writing, talking, laughing, teaching. I am occasionally aware of him.

Every once in a while, I find myself speaking to him in my mind.

*That's a siren—my skin always prickles when I hear a siren. Green beans taste green. Don't mind Nell; she only barks when she's afraid. Walking does feel pretty good, though it's not flying. TV?—Noise. Just lots of noise.*

And so it goes, with me more aware than usual of the shape and texture of my world, its music, surprises, its moments of grace.

My husband's arm circles my back. I rest my head on his chest and feel his heart beating in my ear. I whisper, "This. Yes, this too."

The next morning, as I wake to the sun's rising over the ocean, I feel the hawk depart. With one breath he is inside me. With the next he is gone.

I bow my head, grateful. I am both emptier and fuller than before.

*Norita Dittberner-Jax*

## MONDAY

In the schoolroom with two clocks,
bird song and gears without a face,

the boys and I are writing. They have stopped
their whines and whys, have settled into

*Where would you live if you could?*
We all write, and it is quiet, the scratches

across paper. The boys stop. Erase. Flick
the dust off and continue in the room of two clocks.

When they finish, they come, one by one
to stand by me. I look up

into their beautiful calm eyes and ask,
*Do you have family in Chicago, in Atlanta, in Miami?*

*on Mars, in the jungle, in Oklahoma? A mother*
*four states away, a father unknown?* They do.

One tells me the weather is perfect in Chicago,
another that you live longer if you live in Rio de Janeiro.

I say, *No, you don't, but do you know the statue*
*of Christ in Rio?* and two of the boys open their arms wide

and smile. When they leave I wonder, did I promise too much with my hope for them?

*Norita Dittberner-Jax*

# THE JAZZ TRUMPETER

*You are not who this country says you are.*
—*Hannibal Lokumbe*

His voice is soft,
and he stops often.
The young black men
around the table
fidget with their braids,
sprawl.

*Doing the right thing*,
he says, *is harder*
*than doing 100 Chinese push-ups*.
A pause for push-ups.
The boys take turns
making the triangle
with their hands on the floor,
getting their chins down
into that triangle.

He wears them down
with his voice,
with his silence. He waits
for them to find their way
and they do: One
tells of the grandmother
related to Ida B. Wells;
another is kin to Leadbelly.
None of these boys
is nothing.

On their faces,
a sense of calm
as if some confusion
has been ordered,
bodies upright,
hands quiet in their laps.

He takes up the trumpet,
the slow wail,
shows them what to do
with sorrow.

*Simm Landres*

# LITTLE BOY IN THE MORNING

Birdsong is deaf to the imprinted shadows
as contortions mock loving
*Kama Sutra* silhouettes

Marbles of fluorescent rain
the size of almonds on
already bones toasted crisp to steam

When the born blind saw light
and the mad made insane
jaundiced buds pulsed

Rising unguarded
on the landscape of mortality

*C. R. Resetarits*

## AUSPICIUM

Birds sky skim as if
*corps de ballet*.
First blush is envy
but find on review,
numbed by numbers
gagged by gaggles,
one bird spotted
who flies wind
the wrong way.
Awkward, unlovely,
a salve all the same
for sore eyes wearied
at the bluing threat,
at dawn's dormers
of blank-parchment.

# CONTRIBUTOR NOTES

*Joe Baumann* is a Ph.D. candidate in English at the University of Louisiana at Lafayette, where he is the editor-in-chief of *Rougarou: An Online Literary Journal*. His work has appeared in the *Hawai'i Review*, *Flashquake*, and numerous other journals, and is forthcoming from *Tulane Review* and *Willow Review*.

*Chrystal Berche* writes. Hard times, troubled times. The lives of her characters are never easy, but then what life is? The story is in the struggle, the journey, the triumphs, and the falls. She writes about artists, musicians, loners, drifters, dreamers, hippies, bikers, truckers, hunters, and all the other things she knows and loves. Sometimes, she writes urban romance; sometimes, aliens crash land near a roadside bar. When she isn't writing, she's taking pictures or curled up with a good book and a kitty on her lap.

*Doug Bolling's* poetry has appeared widely in literary magazines, including *Albatross*, *Illuminations*, *Georgetown Review*, *Water-Stone Review*, *Wallace Stevens Journal*, *Poem*, and *Earthshine*, among others. He has received four Pushcart Prize nominations. He lives outside Chicago in Flossmoor, Illinois and has had a long-standing interest in Zen art and poetry.

*Abigail Carl-Klassen* is an M.F.A. candidate at the University of Texas at El Paso, where she also teaches composition and creative writing. Her work has appeared in *Border Senses* magazine and *New Border Voices: An Anthology* (Texas A&M University Press, 2014). She lives with her husband Jonathan. They are seeking new ways to live out their shared values of spirituality, social justice, and personal and community empowerment in their downtown neighborhood.

*Frank Cavano* is a retired physician whose poetry tends to comment on the spiritual, inspirational, and metaphysical realm. He finds writing to be a joyful and sometimes healing endeavor.

*Noel Conneely* has had poems published in *Lalitamba*, *Yellow Medicine Review*, *Coe Review*, *Main Street Rag*, *Willow Review*, and other publications in Ireland and the U.S. He has taught Irish for many years in Dunlavin.

*Scott David* has published novels, a memoir, and a guide to wine and cocktails, as well as numerous short stories. His stories have appeared most recently in *Evening Street Review*, *Entasis*, and *St. Sebastian Review*. He lives in Boston and Provincetown, Massachusetts.

*Norita Dittberner-Jax* is an award-winning poet and essayist whose work has been widely published in small press magazines. Her work as a writer and teacher with correctional programs has been a major influence in her writing. Her collections of poetry include *The Watch* (Whistling Shade Press, 2008), *Longing for Home* (Pudding House Press, 2008), and *What They Always Were* (New Rivers Press, 1996). Her long essay "The Power of Stone" was published in *Stone Voices* last year. She lives and works in Saint Paul, Minnesota.

*Jamie Donohoe*, whose roller derby sobriquet is Mr. Sparkles, is a teacher, actor, father, and husband. He writes drama and poetry instead of folding laundry. "It's a political thing," he often tells his wife. His writing has most recently appeared in the *Cape Rock*, *Freefall*, and the *William and Mary Review*.

*Patricia Farewell's* work has been published in the *Green Mountains Review*, the *American Poetry Review*, the *Partisan Review*, *Chelsea*, the *New York Quarterly*, and other magazines. Her first book won the Story Line Press Frederick Morgan Poetry Prize.

*Michael Fessler* is an American writer and teacher who resides in Japan. His poems and stories have appeared in numerous publications. He is the author of *The Sweet Potato Sutra* (Bottle Rockets Press, 2004).

*Clifford Paul Fetters'* poetry is published or forthcoming in *Main Street Rag*, *Cross Currents*, the *Oxford American*, *Poetry East*, *Appalachia*, the *New York Review of Books*, the *Seattle Review*, the *Willow Review*, *5AM*, *William and Mary Review*, *Ibbetson Street Press*, the *Wisconsin Review*, and many others. He lives in Miami with his writes-like-a-dream wife, Debra Dean.

*Michael Findlay* is currently a director of Acquavella Galleries and has been an art dealer in New York since 1964. In the 1960's he exhibited and published poetry. With poets such as Anne Waldman and Gerard Malanga, he read at Judson Memorial Church and other venues. In the 1970s, Findlay attended workshops with Jean Valentine, June Jordan, and Kenneth Koch. He has written poetry continuously since then but submitted none for publication. His writings were included in *The Expert and the Object* (Oxford University Press, 2004). His book *The Value of Art* (Prestel, 2012) has been translated into German, Spanish, Japanese and Korean.

*Nate Fisher* is an instructor in English Composition and Rhetoric at Southern Illinois University-Edwardsville. He has published both poems and essays concerning the philosophy of mind. He devotes his time to writing commentaries on the Vedic texts and contemplating the 'which from which there is no whicher.' He would like to assure those who are struggling that all of it is only a big play and just to play along.

*Allen Forrest* has created cover art and illustrations for literary publications, including *New Plains Review*, *Pilgrimage Press*, the *MacGuffin*, *Blotterature*, and *Gargoyle* magazines. His paintings have been commissioned and are on display in the Bellevue College Foundation's permanent art collection. Forrest's expressive drawing and painting style is a mix of Avant-Garde, Expressionism, and Post-Impressionist elements, reminiscent of Van Gogh. He creates emotion on canvas.

*Stuart Friebert* is the author of *Speak Mouth to Mouth* (WordTechCommunications, 2009), his thirteenth book of poems. His eighth volume of translations, in co-translation with the author, is *The Swing in the Middle of Chaos: Selected Poems of Sylvia Fischerova* (Bloodaxe Books, 2010). He has also published a number of stories and memoir pieces.

*Patricia George* is a piano accompanist for high school choirs in a small town in California. She has a B.A. in piano performance and a teaching credential from Fresno State University. She has taught public school in Colorado and in California. She holds post graduate credits in graphic and fine arts, and has worked as a graphic artist. You can find her published poetry in *Anderbo*, *Red Booth*, *Inner Art Journal*, and *Thoughtsmith*.

*Fran Isaacs Gilmore* writes from Philadelphia about nature, social concerns, and spiritual matters. She is a retired industrial hygienist. She teaches *yoga* to people in recovery and a class on emotional healing in a maximum security men's prison.

*Gene Goldfarb* began writing many years ago, gave it up to be a judge for over 30 years, and returned to writing through volunteer work. His poems have recently appeared in *Cliterature*, *Empty Sink*, *River & South Review*, *Annapurna*, *Stoneboat*, *Livid Squid*, *A Narrow Fellow*, *SLANT*, and *Thin Air*.

*David L. Gourdine* is a New York City-based photographer: "When the memory is lovelier than the moment."

*John Grey* is an Australian born poet. His writings have recently been published in *International Poetry Review*, *Sanskrit*, and the science fiction anthology *Futuredaze* (Underwords Press, 2013) His work is forthcoming in *Clackamas Literary Review*, *New Orphic Review*, and *Nerve Cowboy*.

*Kathleen Gunton* began publishing poetry and photography after graduating from California State Universty, Long Beach. Recent cover art publications include *Tiferet*, *Art & Letters*, and *Thema*. Her poetry has appeared in *Sojourners*, *Perceptions*, and the William Stafford anthology, *A Ritual to Read Together* (Woodley Press, 2013). Find out more at www.kathleengunton.blogspot.com.

*T.A. Hunley* studied Western Philosophy, East Asian Religion, and English and is currently an English Composition instructor at Marshall University in Huntington, West Virginia. She is a writer, musician, and visual artist who seeks to challenge traditional boundaries of individual modes of artistic expression for the sake of truth.

*Monika John* has recently published poems in *Sampad*, *Buddhist Poetry Review*, *Presence*, *Fungi*, *Urthona Magazine*, *Penwood Review*, *Sathya Sai Newsletters*, and *QuietShorts*. Her work is forthcoming in *Scheherazade's Bequest* and *Crone*. She practiced law in California before moving to an island in the Pacific Northwest.

*Jacqueline Jules* is the author of the poetry chapbook, *Field Trip to the Museum* (Finishing Line Press, 2014). Her poetry has appeared in numerous publications including *Soundings Review*, *Imitation Fruit*, *Calyx*, *Connecticut River Review*, and *Pirene's Fountain*. She is also the author of two dozen books for young readers including *Zapato Power* (Albert Whitman, 2010) and *No English* (Mitten Press, 2007). Visit her online at www.jacquelinejules.com.

*Katrina Kent* has recently been published in *Haunted Waters Press* and other literary journals. She is currently working towards a creative writing degree at the New Hampshire Institute of Art.

*K. Prasad Kumariya* enjoyed the blessing of monastic life before working in biochemistry and science publishing. These days, he enjoys living in the Connecticut Valley near the Massachusetts-Vermont border. He pursues a love of Indian music, while working on a collection of spiritual essays, allegories, and anecdotes.

*Simm Landres* is a native New Yorker, lives in Virginia, and is the father of two. His writings have appeared in *Poem*, *California Quarterly*, *Euphony*, *Snake Nation Review*, and *Little Star*.

*Charlene Langfur* is an organic gardener, a rescue-dog lover, a college teacher, and an S.U. Graduate Writing Fellow. Her poems have appeared in the *Adirondack Review*, *Poetry East*, and *Literal Latte*, among others. Her most recent publications include SUNY's *Blueline*, *Green Mountains Review*, and *Room*.

*Lyn Lifshin* is the author of *Another Woman Who Looks Like Me* (Black Sparrow Press, 2006) and the prize-winning book about the short-lived but beautiful race horse Ruffian, called *The Licorice Daughter: My Year With Ruffian* (Texas Review Press, 2006). Other recent books include *Before It's Light* (Black Sparrow Press, 1999) and *Cold Comfort* (Black Sparrow Press, 1997). www.lynlifshin.com

*Benjamin Nash* has published a few poems in the *Christian Science Monitor*, *Flare*, *Vine Leaves Literary Journal*, *Pilgrimage*, *Literary Juice*, *Red River Review*, and others. Some years ago he studied to be a professor in political science.

*Ayaz Daryl Nielsen* is a poet, father, husband, veteran, x-roughneck (as on oil rigs), and x-hospice nurse. He is currently the editor/custodian of print pub *bear creek haiku* (25 years and over 100 issues). Collections of his poetry include *Concentric Penumbras of the Heart* (CreateSpace, 2012) and *haiku tumbleweeds still tumbling* (CreateSpace, 2012). His blog is bearcreekhaiku.blogspot.com (such fun). Considerable blame should be given to his having a B.A. in English from the University of Wisconsin—Eau Claire.

*Barry W. North* is a sixty-eight-year-old retired refrigeration mechanic. Since his retirement in 2007, he has been nominated twice for a Pushcart Prize, won the 2010 A. E. Coppard Prize for Fiction, and won Honorable Mention in the 2011 Allen Ginsberg Poetry Awards. His work has appeared or is forthcoming in the *Paterson Literary Review*, *Slipstream*, and others. www.barrynorth.org

*Judith Tate O'Brien* has published numerous individual poems, as well as three collections—one of them co-authored with Jane Taylor, *By the Grace of Ghosts* (Village Books Press, 2003). Her latest book, *Crossing a Different Bridge* (Mongrel Empire Press, 2010), is a prose-and-poetry memoir. She is 83 and lives in a retirement center.

*Kenneth O'Keefe* is a retired public school teacher. He has now found the solitude that allows him to pursue a dream he had in his youth. As a young person he discovered how art—more specifically writing—transports us beyond the confines of self and time. While engaged in writing a little story or poem, hours became either suspended or compressed to where they passed as quickly as minutes; thoughts that focused on selfish needs often disappeared. This early experience of transcendence through art was in many ways similar to prayer. To have again the opportunity to live it is a blessing.

*Charlotte F. Otten's* poems have appeared in journals as diverse as *Agenda*, *Southern Humanities Review*, *Poems from Aberystwyth*, the *Healing Muse*, and *Yale Journal for Humanities in Medicine*. She is also the author of a book *The Flying Mouse* (Bunker Hill Publishing, 2014).

*Raul Palma* is a Ph.D. student at the University of Nebraska-Lincoln. His work has appeared or is forthcoming in *Saw Palm*, *Midwestern Gothic*, *NANO*, *Naugatuck River Review*, and others. Originally from South Florida, he lives with his wife and daughter in Lincoln, Nebraska.

*Airica Parker's* poems have appeared most recently in the *Fiddlehead Review* and *Skidrow Penthouse*. The poems featured here come from her current manuscript *Body Bridge*, a collection that seeks common ground. To celebrate poets, poetry, and human connection, Parker founded the community project Postcard Poems on Facebook. A performer, instructor, and healing artist, she makes her home in Colorado. Learn more at www.airicaparker.com.

*Margreta von Pein* is a freelance writer, living in the San Francisco East Bay area. She hikes, sails, and often travels, single and deaf, to countries where she doesn't know the language.

*Susan Azar Porterfield* is the author of two books of poetry: *In the Garden of Our Spines* (Mayapple Press, 2004) and *Kibbe* (Mayapple Press, 2012). She has also published a chapbook, *Beirut Redux* (Finishing Line Press, 2008). She is a Professor of English at Rockford College.

*Christopher Presfield* is the author of *Dawn in the Big House* (Pygmy Forest, 2006) and *South* (Pygmy Forest, 2010). His work also appears in journals such as *Alaska Quarterly Review*, *Poetry*, *Rattle*, *Briar Cliff Review*, and *Poet Lore*.

*Vanessa Raney* is an American living in Croatia (and traveling). For a detailed list of her publications, please go to http://vanessa-raney.blogspot.com. Her art poem series can be found at http://vanessa-raney2artpoemseries.blogspot.com.

*Dian Duchin Reed* is the author of *Medusa Discovers Styling Gel* (Finishing Line Press, 2009). Recent poems appear in *Prairie Schooner*, *Poet Lore*, *Nimrod International Journal*, and *Poetry East*. She has been the recipient of a Sundberg Family grant for literary criticism, the Mel Tuohey Award for writing excellence, and the Mary Lonnberg Smith Award in Poetry.

*C. R. Resetarits'* poetry has recently appeared in *New Writing*, *Kindred*, *Post Road*, *dirtcake*, and the anthologies *Lines Underwater* (TyburnTree, 2013) and *Drawn to Marvel: Poems from the Comic Books* (Minor Arcana Press, 2014).

*Ryan Rickrode* grew up in central Pennsylvania, where he studied creative writing and religion at Susquehanna University. In 2013 he completed his M.F.A. in creative writing at the University of Montana. His work has recently appeared in *Identity Theory*.

*M. J. Roberts* has won awards for her poetry, short stories, and plays from American Pen Women, Charlotte Rep, the City of Los Angeles, and others. More than ten of her plays have been produced in Los Angeles and other parts of the country. She is the author of the poetry collection *Sound of No Sound* ( Tuna Beach Press, 2012). She is an Associate Professor at Santa Monica College, where she teaches writing.

*Paul B. Roth's* most recent collection of poetry is *Words the Interrupted Speak* (March Street Press, 2011). He is editor and publisher of the *Bitter Oleander Press* and resides in upstate New York's village of Fayetteville.

*Stephanie Renée dos Santos* is a fiction and freelance writer, and yoga instructor. She leads Saraswati Writing and Yoga Workshops in Brazil and the United States. Workshop practices are based on Kum Nye Yoga by Tarthang Tulku of the Nyingma Tibetan Buddhist tradition, Vedanta Yoga as taught by Sivananda Saraswati and Satyananda Saraswati, and the Amherst Writers & Artists Method. She's published fiction in *American Athenaeum* and *Lalitamba*. Currently, she is working on her first historical novel, *Cut from the Earth*. www.stephaniereneedossantos.com.

*Matt Schumacher* has published poems in *Cincinnati Review*, the *Fiddlehead Review*, *Fourteen Hills*, and *Green Mountain Review's 25 Year Poetry Retrospective* issue. He serves as poetry editor for a journal of New Fabulism called *Phantom Drift*. His books include *Spilling the Moon* (Wordcraft of Oregon, 2008) and *The Fire Diaries* (Wordcraft of Oregon, 2010).

*Purvi Shah* seeks to inspire change through her work as a non-profit consultant, anti-violence advocate, and writer. She is the winner of the inaugural SONY South Asian Excellence Award for Social Service for her work fighting violence against women, and recently directed *Together We Are New York: Asian Americans Remember and Re-Vision 9/11*. Her debut book *Terrain Tracks* (New Rivers Press, 2006), garnered the Many Voices Project prize and was nominated for the Asian American Writers' Workshop Members' Choice Award. Find out more at www.purvipoets.net and www.huffingtonpost.com/purvi-shah.

*Mark Dennis Smith* works for the Postal Service in the Portland Area with his wife and family. He loves reading Dante, Emily Dickinson, and William Blake. He also likes cats, Coca-Cola, and movies—but only good movies.

*Sarah Spivack* enjoys baking and having fun with her family, when she is not writing. She is a freshman in high school who is currently working on several short story collections and a novel. She lives in Sacramento, California with her parents and brother.

*Bonnie Stanard* is a writer of novels, short stories, and poems with credits in numerous publications such as *Slipstream*, *Knock*, and *Harpur Palate*. Her three antebellum novels are available at various venues online. Her blog can be found at http://writepersona.blogspot.com. She lives in Columbia, South Carolina with her husband.

*Diane Vreuls* has published a novel, a collection of short stories, a children's book, and a book of poems, as well as work in such magazines as *Commonweal* and the *New Yorker*. Professor of Creative Writing at Oberlin College, she has also pursued studies at St. Mary Seminary in Cleveland. Retired from teaching, she now serves as a hospital chaplain and minister to the homebound in her parish.

*Keir Weimer* is a twenty-nine-year-old who was recently released from a New York State prison. He served three-and-a-half years for his responsibility in a fatal boating accident that occurred in 2006. Weimer wrote an anthology of short stories about his experience, observations, and lessons while incarcerated. *Just Another Day* is one of these pieces dealing with the daily struggles of life in captivity. In addition to his work as an author, Weimer is an active keynote speaker, advancing the powerful message contained in his story to youth in a variety of settings. He is also an entrepreneur and recently founded a real estate investment and holding firm.

*Katherine West* is a poet, teacher, and editor. In 2005 she founded Green Fuse Poetic Arts Association, a non-profit organization dedicated to nourishing poetry and connecting grass roots poets with their community through publishing, readings, and workshops. She has published two poetry collections, *Scimitar Dreams* (Green Fuse Community Press, 2006) and *The Bone Train* (Howling Dog Press, 2008).

*Kelley Jean White* is a member of the Religious Society of Friends and a pediatrician. She worked in inner-city Philadelphia for nearly thirty years and now works in rural New Hampshire. Her poems have appeared in journals including *Exquisite Corpse*, *Rattle*, and *JAMA*. Her most recent books are *Toxic Environment* (Boston Poet Press, 2008) and *Two Birds in Flame* (Beech River Books, 2010). Many of the poems included are inspired by the Shaker community at Canterbury, NH.

*Barbara Wuest* has published poems in *Wisconsin Academy Review*, the *Paris Review*, the *Cape Rock*, *Dogwood*, *Western Ohio Journal*, *CrossCurrents*, *First Things*, *Christianity and Literature*, *Cincinnati Poetry Review*, *Laurel Review*, the *Beloit Poetry Journal*, *Vineyard*, and others. She holds an M.F.A. Poetry from U.C. Irvine and an M.A. Theology from University of San Diego.

*Gabriele Zuokaite* is a freelance novelist and poet from Lithuania. A high school senior, she is trying to develop herself as an independent contemporary writer. Her main topics are diversity, talent's sufferings, loneliness, youth's aspirations, and incertitude.

# LALITAMBA SARANAM

*P.O. Box 131, Planetarium Station; New York, NY 10024*

*Lalitamba* partners with Lalitamba Saranam, a holistic homeless shelter in New York City. Through years of working with people in need of permanent housing, we understand how stressful the situation can be. Lalitamba Saranam offers all the comforts of home to women in transition, including survivors of domestic violence, runaway youth, and senior citizens. ***To make a tax-deductible donation to the shelter, please send a check to Lalitamba Saranam at the above address.*** Your generosity makes it all possible. Thank you!

**www.threejewelsrefuge.org**

# SUBSCRIBE

*P.O. Box 131, Planetarium Station; New York, NY 10024*

_____$12 One-Year Subscribtion (one annual issue)

_____$20 Two-Year Subscription (two annual issues)

Please add $4.95 for postage and handling and enclose a check written to *Lalitamba*.

Begin my subscription with issue number _____

Name_______________________________________________

Address_____________________________________________

City, State, Zip_______________________________________

Please send a gift subscription to:

Begin the subscription with issue number _____

Name_______________________________________________

Address_____________________________________________

City, State, Zip_______________________________________

www.ingramcontent.com/pod-product-compliance
Lightning Source LLC
Chambersburg PA
CBHW051822040426
42447CB00006B/324